A STUDY OF 1 & 2 THESSALONIANS FOR TEEN GIRLS

{FAITHFUL ONE}

AMY-JO GIRARDIER

LifeWay Press®
Nashville, Tennessee

© 2014 LifeWay Press®
Reprinted Nov. 2014

No part of this work may be reproduced or transmitted in any form or by any means, electronic or mechanical, including photocopying and recording, or by any information storage or retrieval system, except as may be expressly permitted in writing by the publisher.

Requests for permission should be addressed in writing to
LifeWay Press®, One LifeWay Plaza, Nashville, TN 37234-0144.

ISBN: 978-1-4300-3239-7
Item Number: 005646506

Dewey Decimal Classification Number: 248.83
Subject Heading: GIRLS \ CHRISTIAN LIFE \ BIBLE. N.T. THESSALONIANS

Printed in the United States of America

We believe that the Bible has God for its author; salvation for its end; and truth, without any mixture of error, for its matter and that all Scripture is totally true and trustworthy. To review LifeWay's doctrinal guideline, please visit *www.lifeway.com/doctrinalguideline.*

Student Ministry Publishing
LifeWay Church Resources
One LifeWay Plaza
Nashville, TN 37234-0144

Table of Contents

About the Author

Amy-Jo Girardier is the Girls Minister at Brentwood Baptist in Brentwood, TN. She has been serving in this role for 11 years and still can't believe this is what she gets to do for a job! Originally from Springfield, Illinois, Amy-Jo graduated from Southwest Baptist University and attended Southwestern Baptist Theological Seminary to pursue a Masters in Christian Education. She is the founding editor of *www.girlsminister.com*, a website created to connect and resource girls ministers, moms, and youth workers engaged in the girls ministry conversation. Amy-Jo is a contributor to *youthministry360.com*, and *faithvillage.com*. In addition to ministry, Amy-Jo loves using technology, passing on her love of technology to others, drinking coffee, running, serving with her husband Darrel, loving on her son Scout, and chill-axing with her Boston Terrier Diesel.

Special Thanks

Thank you to my husband, Darrel, and son, Scout, for the many sacrifices you made so I could participate in this. Thanks to my first girls minister, my mom Connie Jo Morgan, for preparing meals, praying, and taking care of my family when I pulled late nights. Thanks to my student ministry team for their support (Linc, Chris, Aaron, Julia, Carol, and Abbie). Thanks to my pastor Mike Glenn, who prays for me and cheers me on. Thanks to Matt Purdom, Kairos Discipleship Pastor, who gave insight on the Greek work in this study.

This study would not have been possible without the constant prayer support from what I affectionately call "TEAM AJ". There were people from around the world praying for me as I wrote, for my editorial team as they edited, for my video team as they produced, and they will continue to pray for you as you study this with your group. TEAM AJ: Mike Glenn, Scott and Paige Drennan, Lori Beth Horton, The Crosby Family, Bonita Wilson, Marty Girardier, Lorri Steiner, Aaron and Kelsey Kunz, Keely and Michael Boggs, Rachel Chan, Jen and Greg Pinkner, Stacey and Mark Morgan, Karla Worley, Amy and Aaron Bryant, Mary Lindsey Blanton, JoEllen Taylor, Clay Huddleston, Evan Kunz, Rene Cook, Austen Barrett, and Tiffany Evins.

Special thanks to my 6th grade Sunday School class as they "tested" out some of the lessons. And thanks to all the girls and leaders at Brentwood Baptist Church who were in my heart as I wrote this resource to be used for God's glory.

And of course, thanks to the best editor in the world, Alicia Claxton. Thanks to Mike Wakefield and the LifeWay Student team for their support, hard work, and for believing in me.

About the Study

This eight-session resource will lead girls through an in-depth study of 1 and 2 Thessalonians. They will examine biblical context and a multitude of spiritual truths in these letters from the apostle Paul. Girls will discover more about the character of Christ and come to know Him as the Faithful One who reigns supreme. They will be challenged to live as faithful followers of Jesus in a world desperate for the gospel.

We recommend offering an initial introductory session so girls can get more information about the focus of the study and details for weekly group meetings. Consider showing the Intro Video included on the Leader Kit DVD to introduce the author and give an overview of the resource.

How to Use

In this book, you will find content for weekly group studies, daily personal studies, and leader guide notes in the back. Each week is organized into the following sections:

✤ Scripture page
This is the first page of each session and is designed to help girls interact with the focal chapter. The page includes space for them to underline, circle, and draw symbols in the margins as instructed throughout the week.

✤ Intro
This page is designed to open the session with illustrations and object lessons.

✤ Between the Lines
This section contains the bulk of the group Bible study, including historical context, word studies, and discussion questions.

✤ Reflect and Respond
This section is designed to help girls apply what they have learned.

✤ Share Your Story
We want to encourage girls to share on social media what they are learning and thinking about as they journey through this study. For those who don't use social media, there is space provided to write responses to each challenge.

✤ Going Deeper
There are five days of additional personal study material that will help girls dig deeper into the truths found in each chapter of 1 and 2 Thessalonians. We encourage you to talk about this material each week as you meet in the group setting.

SESSION I

The Imprint of Christ

1 THESSALONIANS 1:1-10

1 Paul, Silvanus, and Timothy: To the church of the Thessalonians in God the Father and the Lord Jesus Christ. Grace to you and peace. 2 We always thank God for all of you, remembering you constantly in our prayers. 3 We recall, in the presence of our God and Father, your work of faith, labor of love, and endurance of hope in our Lord Jesus Christ, 4 knowing your election, brothers loved by God. 5 For our gospel did not come to you in word only, but also in power, in the Holy Spirit, and with much assurance. You know what kind of men we were among you for your benefit, 6 and you became imitators of us and of the Lord when, in spite of severe persecution, you welcomed the message with joy from the Holy Spirit. 7 As a result, you became an example to all the believers in Macedonia and Achaia. 8 For the Lord's message rang out from you, not only in Macedonia and Achaia, but in every place that your faith in God has gone out. Therefore, we don't need to say anything, 9 for they themselves report what kind of reception we had from you: how you turned to God from idols to serve the living and true God 10 and to wait for His Son from heaven, whom He raised from the dead—Jesus, who rescues us from the coming wrath.

Intro

It's hard to imagine a world without instant communication like texting or social media, but just for fun, let's pretend that those methods of communication don't exist right now. What if your only options for sending a message were:

- ✦ A message in a bottle (a note sealed in a bottle and left floating in the ocean for someone to find)
- ✦ A message by airmail (a packet that is sent from one person to another by plane)
- ✦ A message by courier (a messenger sent to deliver the message personally)

How would the method of communication impact the message you wanted to communicate?

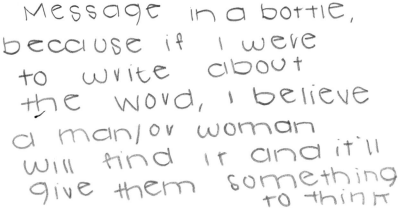

Message in a bottle, because if I were to write about the word, I believe a man/or woman will find it and it'll give them something to think about.

How do you prefer to receive messages and encouragement from others?
- **A. A direct message on Twitter**
- **B. A "like" or "comment" on Instagram**
- **C. A text message**

Look at the text messages you sent most recently. Imagine you had to send those words by way of a message in a bottle. Now imagine how difficult it might be for someone other than the recipient to pick up your message and try to decipher it. Since the note you sent was intended to be read by someone specific, anyone else reading it would miss the full intention and significance of your words without some context (the "who, what, when, where, and why" of a message).

We must approach this study with a similar perspective. As we get ready to dig into chapter 1 of 1 Thessalonians, there are a few things we need to take note of if we are to grasp the depth and richness of the words. Otherwise, it will feel like we've just picked up a message in a bottle or reached into a stranger's mailbox and started reading a letter with no context. Let's start with some background information to get a clearer picture of Paul's letter to this group of believers.

Between the Lines

The apostle Paul wrote this letter to a group of new believers in Thessalonica. It will become very evident as you read that the Thessalonians had found a very special place in Paul's heart. You'll see strong phrases such as, "we were torn away from you in person, not in heart," and "we long to see you," used throughout the passages. Paul had a significant message to share with a group of people who had come to mean a great deal to him in a short amount of time. (See the Historical Context box for more insight.) As I've thought about the words Paul wrote, it has been helpful to compare the time he spent with the Thessalonians to the equivalent of a short-term mission trip. Sadly, this particular "mission trip" abruptly ended with rioting by unbelievers who forced Paul and his companions out of town. The amount of time may have been short, but the impact was huge.

Though Paul was physically in another part of Greece, his love for the Thessalonians and his desire to see them grow spiritually weighed heavy on his heart. I imagine that he could not get their faces out of his mind as he prayed for them diligently. Prompted by the Holy Spirit, he began writing the letter we now know as 1 Thessalonians. From the very beginning, it is apparent Paul had some key points that he wanted to communicate to his friends and fellow believers in Thessalonica.

As we read God's Word together, I want you to interact with the text. Use the Scripture page at the beginning of each session (p. 7 for Session 1) to underline, circle, and draw as we dig deeper into each passage. **Read chapter 1 together now.**

Underline verse 5. Notice the way Paul alludes back to the time when he and his companions first visited Thessalonica and shared the gospel with them. **Read Acts 17:2-4.**

Write _Acts 17:2-4_ in the margin next to verse 5 as a cross reference with insight into Paul's original missionary journey to Thessalonica.

What message had Paul originally preached to the Thessalonians?

Christ had to suffer to rise from the dead.

How did the people respond to this message?

Some of the Jews joined paul & silas Also, a large # of God fearing Greeks.

HISTORICAL CONTEXT

Academic researchers have debated just how short Paul's time in Thessalonica was. Based on Acts 17, it documents three weeks with the Thessalonian believers before Paul and his friends were forced out of town. Other commentaries have extended his time to as long as six months.[1]

CULTURAL CONTEXT

Thessalonica was a major city in Macedonia that became an important trade route in the Roman Empire during this time frame. The culture was decidedly pagan and immoral. There was much persecution for those who claimed the resurrected Christ as their Lord and Savior. Paul did not want these new believers to get discouraged or be deceived as they lived out their faith in this dark culture, so he wrote letters to keep them focused on the gospel message.

WORD STUDY

Mimetes: Greek word for imitators; we get our English word *mimic* from this Greek word. Also translated into our English word *follower*.[2]

WORD STUDY

Tupos: Greek word for example; translation literally means "the indention left from a strike, or a blow" or "to make an imprint." We get our English word, *type* from this Greek word.[3]

The message Paul preached was the resurrected Christ! Now in his letter to the Thessalonians, Paul gave them a picture for the kind of people they were becoming known as because of the transformational work of Christ in their lives.

Read verse 6 and circle the word *imitators*.

The picture Paul was conveying is a powerful one. For *imitators*, he used the Greek word *mimetes*, which is where we get our English word, *mimic*. Now the thing that blew my mind as I was studying this passage is that *mimetes* is also the Greek word translated into our English word *follower*. I don't know about you, but I hear the phrase "Christ-follower" so often in the church that it's easy to lose sight of what it really means. These Thessalonians were understanding for the first time what it meant to mimic Christ and to follow His example in every area of their lives.

Describe the character and attitudes of one who mimics Christ with his or her life.

Any thing they do or say is to praise the Lord above.

Unfortunately in our postmodern culture, to follow Christ has taken on different meanings. Some people think being a "good, moral person" is what it means to follow Christ. Others think that going to church on Sundays is following Christ. But Scripture presents a very different picture of what it truly means to pattern our lives after Jesus.

Read verse 7 and draw a box around the word *example*.

Paul painted another rich picture in verse 7 by using the word *example*. The Greek word used is *tupos*. There are a few different translations of this word, but one means "the indention left from a strike, or a blow" or "to make an imprint." We get our English word *type* from this Greek word.[4] It's the idea of something like a typewriter key striking a page and leaving the imprint of a particular letter or letters on the page for everyone to read. In Paul's day it would be like making a stamp in clay. He was describing for the Thessalonians what it meant to live their lives in such a way that they left an indention—a TYPE—that people saw and recognized as a Christ-follower. Paul reiterated this picture for his young pastor friend Timothy when he said in 1 Timothy 4:12, *You should be an example to the believers.*

Write *1 Timothy 4:12* in the margin next to verse 7 as a cross reference where Paul used the same Greek word for *example*.

[Handwritten at top:] May 4th, 2020

[Handwritten in right margin:] Don't let anyone look down on you because you are young, but set an example for the believers in speech, in life, in love, in faith & in purity.

Based on this message to the Thessalonians, I walk away asking some key questions that lay the groundwork for what it truly means to be a faithful one who follows **THE Faithful One**. Paul made it abundantly clear that our lives leave marks or "examples" that identify who and what we are following. May we leave an imprint of Christ everywhere we go!

Have you made a personal commitment to follow Christ? If so, when? If not, what is holding you back?

[Handwritten:] I'm trying. I'm honestly really struggling. I make an excuse to live in the world

What are some ways in which the Holy Spirit is working in you and making you more like Christ?

[Handwritten:] I honestly haven't let Him. I'm not portraying not w/ Him. God very well, God.

In what areas do you struggle most to be faithful?

[Handwritten:] Everywhere. I sin constantly. I'm a cruel person

If your life's story was typed out for the world to read, what message(s) do you think would be communicated most vividly?

[Handwritten:] Still trying to be ok, come back in an hour.

Because social media is such a great tool for sharing our stories, I want to encourage you to post what you are learning as we journey through this study. You'll find a section called "Share Your Story" at the end of each session with a specific challenge for that day. As you share, use #FaithfulOne. If you don't use social media, there is space provided to write your response.

SHARE YOUR STORY

Challenge: *The apostle Paul understood that in order to BE a faithful follower, we need to embrace the Faithful One named Christ. Share what having a relationship with Jesus means to you.*

[Handwritten:] I don't want to hurt so much anymore & I know God loves me and wants to help me through this. #FaithfulOne

As you begin each day of personal study, it's important to recognize that we are not just going deeper for the sake of knowledge. We are coming to God with a desire to know Him more and to have our hearts molded by the truth of His Word. Start this time with prayer. Prayer is simply an honest conversation between your heart and God. Your most authentic prayer on some days might start like this: "Jesus, I'm tired today but I know I need You in my life. Capture my attention as I read Your Word. Amen." Find a place where you will not be distracted. Put your devices on "Do Not Disturb" mode and show up ready to meet with God.

Whatever it is that you need to say to Him, I invite you to do that now by writing a prayer in the space provided.

Recently, I was cleaning out boxes from my childhood room and stumbled across an old group note collectively written by about seven of my friends during a study hall. This particular study hall was very strict and had a zero tolerance policy on talking—but we could write and pass notes all day long. It was kind of like looking at a group text, but the value of having it in a note form with our own handwriting and doodles made it priceless.

I want you to consider doing something similar with the two letters called 1 and 2 Thessalonians. You are not just an observer or a third party that has intercepted a message from Paul to a group of believers in Thessalonica. Scripture is God's message and He has something for you to hear as well! Each session will include a page with the chapter written out. Use this page (p. 7 in this session) to interact with the passage you are studying. I will guide you through some questions and activities so you can participate in the learning process. Think of yourself as one of the friends in my group note adding your questions, doodles, and comments in the margins. Not only will you get to see some cool visuals jump out in each chapter, you'll also have a keepsake of what God taught you as you read His Word.

Now take a moment to read 1 Thessalonians chapter one aloud or quietly to yourself. Once you've read through it, focus in on the following words and phrases.

 Underline <u>we always thank God</u> in verse 2. Next, draw a turkey in the margin near the word _thank_. When you think of a turkey, what holiday comes to mind? Thanksgiving! One of the key themes of this letter is encouragement. Paul wanted these new believers to know he was thankful for them because he could see the evidence of Christ at work in them. From now on, when you see something about giving thanks, you "turkey" that phrase and look for what Paul was drawing their attention to. More than likely, it will be the activity of Christ in their lives.

In verse 3, Paul primarily thanked God for three things: the *faith*, *love*, and *hope* the Thessalonians had experienced because of Christ. These three themes (faith, love, and hope) will come up again and again so, yes, we have pictures for them as well. Let's use a cross for faith, a heart for love, and sunshine for hope. **Go ahead and draw those images in the margin next to verse 3.**

Through Paul's description of the Thessalonians, we discover that these three attributes defined them. They had become famous outside their own town because of their faith, love, and hope. For now, let's focus on the last word...*hope*. The kind of hope described here is a sure thing, yet based on a reality not yet seen. These early Christians clung to the hope that Christ would one day return even as they lived in the reality of the "not yet." We know that same kind of hope today.

Read verses 8-9. Draw a cross, heart, and sunshine in the margin to highlight the fact that their faith, love, and hope were making an impact on others.

According to verse 9, how did the Thessalonians respond to the gospel message Paul had originally preached?

Why do you think those actions were significant?

SHARE YOUR STORY

Challenge: *What would it look like for your life to reflect the brilliance of Christ and point our culture to His faithfulness? Finish this prayer: Lord, help me to point others to You by...*

#FaithfuLOne

Each day we will read the chapter for the week again with fresh eyes. Continue using page 7 in your book to interact with the text as we focus on specific verses.

Read 1 Thessalonians chapter 1 now and circle any words or phrases that catch your attention. Is there a verse that makes you ask a question as you read it? Go ahead and underline that verse and put a question mark in the margin.

This may be a new way for you to interact with God's Word, but keep in mind that when you go into this time seeking God, you will find Him. The Holy Spirit will be faithful to help you discover truth, examine your own heart, and enjoy His presence.

Here is a glimpse of what interacting with Scripture in this way looks like for me...While I was reading this chapter, verses 2 and 3 stuck out to me. I underlined, "remembering you constantly in our prayers. We recall in the presence of our God..." That prompted me to write this question in the margin: "Who are the people I talk to Jesus about? How often do I mention them in my prayers?" That's a beautiful picture, isn't it? To me, it's such a precious gift to think that other people are talking to Jesus about me, or approaching Him on my behalf at different times. I want to be able to do that as well. As a result of a simple question that came to mind as I read, I started talking to God about the people He brought to my heart's attention. I did not expect to have that experience as I began reading chapter one that day. But what a sweet experience! Now it's your turn.

 Underline the following sentence from verse 6: in spite of severe persecution, you welcomed the message with joy from the Holy Spirit. Over the word _persecution_, draw a bandage to represent the fact that the persecution they endured was not just verbal, but physical.

The Thessalonians lived in a culture where the cost of following Christ was steep. A few years ago, I decided I wanted to visit a place where being a Christian was illegal and persecution like what the early church experienced was still very real. I went with my mother and a mentor who was familiar with the culture of Southeast Asia. We flew in and were immediately told what words we were NOT allowed to use while we were there for fear it could put the Christians and missionaries we were meeting with at extreme risk.

What do you think is the most dangerous word for Christians in Southeast Asia?
   A. Church
   B. God
   C. Prayer
   D. Missionary

Some of the words on the list of "things not to say" were: Christian, church, Jesus, God, prayer, and Bible. But _missionary_ was at the top of the list of extremely volatile words. As I met in secret with pastors and other "M's" (missionaries) to hear about how Christ was at work, the interesting thing I kept hearing over and over again was how THEY were praying for US! They had heard stories of how the church in the West was "sleeping." They had heard about many American Christians who had taken their faith for granted. These Southeast Asian believers were confronted daily with the cost of following Christ while the evidence seemed to indicate we in America thought very seldom about that cost. For many Christ-followers around the world, persecution is real—they meet in secret, hide their Bibles, and speak cautiously. Their jobs, their families and, in some areas, even their lives are at risk because of their faith. And yet…the church in Southeast Asia where we visited was thriving! The government declared Christianity illegal because they were scared of how the gospel transforms lives. The gospel restores people's dignity, it sets people free, and it gives people purpose and courage. As difficult as it is to be a Christ-follower in Southeast Asia, God is doing a mighty work and many are willingly facing each new day believing that whatever happens, He is worth it!

Now that you have a sense of what persecution is like today, let's journey back in time to when the early church was first experiencing it. Put yourself in the shoes (ahem, sandals) of the Thessalonians as you answer the following questions.

What words from chapter 1 of Paul's letter do you think encouraged the Thessalonians the most in the midst of their persecution?

Are you currently experiencing any form of persecution as a result of your faith in Christ? At home, at school, or with friends? Explain.

Write anything that may be hindering you from living with spiritual boldness.

SHARE YOUR STORY

Challenge: *The Thessalonians were examples of faithful imitators of Christ, no matter the cost. Hebrews 13:3 tells us to "Remember the prisoners, as though you were in prison with them, and the mistreated, as though you yourselves were suffering bodily." Today there are still persecuted Christians around the world. Write a message of encouragement to those who have chosen to live out their faith…no matter the cost.*

#FaithfulOne

Begin with a time of prayer to focus your heart. Ask God to show you whatever it is that He wants you to learn, confess, or live out today. Continue using page 7 in your book to interact with the text as we focus on specific verses.

Read 1 Thessalonians chapter 1 again with a fresh perspective. When you get to verse 7, pause at the word example. In the margin next to this verse, draw a footprint to symbolize example.

In our first session, we looked at the Greek word *tupos* used for our word *example* and discovered that the word picture that goes along with it is that of a stamp or typewriter. Today we are going to see another picture this Greek word portrays—a footprint.[5] Paul used the same root word in Philippians 3:17 when he said, *Brothers, join in imitating me, and keep your eyes on those who walk according to the example you have in us* (ESV).

There was a lot of walking done in Paul's day. There were dusty roads and lots of footprints to be seen. Today we typically only see footprints on the beach or in muddy places. We don't usually walk long journeys in places where we can turn and see where we've come from or literally follow in someone's footsteps like you could in Paul's day.

Think about the steps your feet have taken. Draw a footprint to help you process some spiritual application. On the big toe, write one place you have gone that you would love to go back to again. Inside the middle toe, write one place you did not like going. On the heel of the foot, write about a time when you "put your foot down" and took a stand in a difficult situation.

I have a love/hate relationship with my feet. I love to run, but I have foot problems that cause me a lot of pain when I run. I played collegiate soccer for four years and experienced some pretty extensive damage to my already bad feet. I was told then that one day I would have to have surgery. That day came in 2006 and 2008. I had bones cut, shifted, and bolted together in some form or fashion in both of my feet. After the first surgery, I was unable to walk for nine weeks. The first time I put my foot down after surgery, I couldn't remember how to walk. We take walking for granted. I wrote a letter to myself during this whole endeavor so I wouldn't forget all that God taught me about walking. *"Dear AJ, You just had surgery. You have horrible feet. Your feet got out of line because you took poorly formed feet and pushed them to their limits with track in high school and college soccer. Now as an adult they won't let you do what you need them to do. You had a hard time moving from pain to surgery to healing to walking forward again. You couldn't remember how to walk. Someone actually told you what you were doing wrong and that you were forgetting to walk heel to toe. It was quite a hard time for you to reteach your muscles and endure limping publicly."* The phases I went through in this process were as follows:

+ **Ignoring:** I didn't want to deal with the pain so I just kept pushing through.
+ **Correcting:** I went to extremes in college even with physical therapists creating a bulky plastic protector that was taped to my foot instead of surgery that was needed.
+ **Numbness:** My foot would go numb from bones pinching on nerves.
+ **Surgery:** It became mandatory to have surgery to realign and remove some bones.
+ **Crippling:** I had a time of complete immobility where I had to use crutches.
+ **Baby steps:** I had to relearn how to walk and ended up limping for quite awhile.
+ **Practice:** I had to practice and continue to walk forward one step at a time.

To me this was as much a faith journey as it was a physical journey. As I wondered if I would ever be able to take a normal step again, I spent many moments in prayer. It became an illustration of my own walk with God. It's healthy to pause and consider how our walk with Christ is unfolding. Here are some questions to help you consider your own walk of faith.

Where are you on your faith walk? Is there a spiritual question or sin that is crippling your relationship with God? Explain.

Are you ignoring your relationship with God? If so, why?

Are you numb spiritually? If so, what is causing that numbness?

Are you stalled or moving forward?

What do your footprints say about the direction you are heading?

A walk with Christ is a process of learning and growing. The question we must all begin with is this: Are you following His lead or have you chosen a different set of footprints to follow?

SHARE YOUR STORY

Challenge: *What would you say to those who may be walking in the footprints you are leaving behind?*

#FaithfulOne

Begin with a time of prayer to focus your heart. Continue using page 7 in your book to interact with the text as we focus on specific verses.

Read 1 Thessalonians chapter 1 again and circle any words or phrases that catch your attention this time around.

Don't give in to the temptation to just skim over the chapter because you've read it several times now. I once heard someone describe God's Word like a diamond. A diamond has many facets and when turned or observed in the light, a different aspect of beauty is discovered. As we search Scripture daily, His light illuminates truths that though we've read them a hundred times before, become fresh and new again. Isn't that exciting? Never underestimate the power of God's Word.

Let's look back at Acts 17:2-4, the cross-reference we looked at in session one to get insight into Paul's first missionary journey to Thessalonica. Go back and read those verses now.

In Acts 17:2-4, Paul uses the word *proclaim*. It is from the Greek word *katangéllō* which means to proclaim or announce publicly.[6] In ancient times this was done by a herald employed by the king or government to make announcements to the people. Paul used the word for proclamation to point to an announcement from his King Jesus that included good news for all people. It's important to remember that the message that was tied to katangéllō was Paul proclaiming what Christ has done, not what he (Paul) had done or not done. He preached about how Christ works. Christ brings life where death has been. Christ breaks the shackles of sin where it once enslaved. When the work of Christ is preached and lived out, then you will experience transformation that people take notice of. This is what was happening among the Thessalonians. It was a published message of Christ's work upon their lives.

 Underline verse 8. Now in the margin, draw the symbol for message, which will be a bullhorn.

Can you imagine how exciting it was to be a Christian in Thessalonica at this time in history? Yes, there was certainly danger. But it was never boring! When they woke up in the morning and set their feet on the ground, they knew Christ was at work and they wanted to be a part of it.

I shared with you about the difficulties I have had with my feet. After I had my son, I didn't have the luxury of letting my feet gear up for the day like I had been doing. As soon as I heard him cry, I had to pop out of bed and get to his room quickly to make sure he had what he needed. I began to dread when my feet would hit the ground because they were hurting so badly. I realized one early morning as I looked at my feet, that the first words out of my heart were words of dread to start the day. It had nothing to do with my son. I just dreaded taking that first, second, and third steps to start my day. God really began to deal with me about this. He laid the Scripture, Isaiah 6:8, on my heart. It's the passage where Isaiah responds to God's call and proclaims, *Here I am. Send me.* I decided that at that moment, I would place that prayer in a visible spot where I would see it every morning and remind myself that I am sent. When my feet touch the floor now, I see: "send me." And the first spot those feet go is into the room of my little boy. And I share with Him the love of Jesus as best as I can. And then the next spot those feet go is to minister to girls and their families at the church where I work. And I share with them the love of Jesus as best as I can. And the next spot those feet go...well that's the exciting part because every day I live with expectation of where He will send me. But I have found what interests people I talk with most, whether it's my hair stylist, my favorite waiter, my friend who is journeying in her investigation with Christ, or random people I interact with while traveling, is a Christ-centered, Christ-proclaiming conversation. They are fascinated with hearing stories about how the Lord is at work in my life and the lives around me. We need to be proclaiming: "See that? That's Christ! That's nothing you or I could have done."

As we conclude today, I want you to begin to exercise your spiritual eyes to see the work of Christ. If you are surrounded by only Christ-followers, then I encourage you to take your feet to some new places. One way to begin to find opportunities to proclaim Christ, is by routinely going to places and cultivating friendships with people God gives you opportunity to connect with. If you are truly living a "Christ-proclaimed" kind of life, then it won't be long before people discover there's something different about you. If you are surrounded by those who are not Christ-followers and they haven't asked you about Christ, that may be an indicator that they aren't seeing the message of Christ preached through your daily walk. It may be that they don't see much of a difference in the way you live your life and the way they live theirs.

Who is God urging you to share His message with through your conversations and actions?

Think of the places you go most often. Are there people there that need to be encouraged spiritually? Are there people there who do not know Christ? Begin to pray for opportunities to make connections with people you interact with about Christ's work.

SHARE YOUR STORY

Challenge: *Where have you seen Christ at work lately? Have you seen Christ restore a broken situation or redeem a broken relationship? Share about that experience.*

#FaithfuLOne

Hello friend. You're back for more! Congratulations on faithfully returning to work on this study each day this week. I hope by now you have a spot or a few distraction free zones you have been frequenting that allow your heart and mind to get on the same page with God. Make sure you shut off those devices and get ready to enjoy your last day in 1 Thessalonians chapter 1. Continue using page 7 to make notes and draw the pictures as we go through.

Start by reading the chapter again. As you come to the last two verses, it is rich with content. Draw a box around the words *turned to God* in verse 9. Off to the side, draw an arrow pointing away from the passage to symbolize turning away from the idols. The word *turned* here means to change one's beliefs.[7] The Thessalonians had once believed in idols and turned from them to embrace the living God!

Next, draw a box around the word *serve* in verse 9. Draw a symbol like a stick figure kneeling with hands raised to illustrate that the Thessalonians no longer bowed to idols but to God. They turned away from dead idols, and were put to work for the living and true God. Their allegiance was to Him and they served His purposes in His kingdom.

Finally, I want you to place a box around the word *wait* in verse 10. Draw a clock.

When was the last time you waited for something? What was it? Draw the type of emotion you associate with waiting in the space below.

When I hear the word *wait*, it often makes me think I have to just sit still. We wait in lines. We sit in restaurant lobbies waiting for our names to be called so we can eat. We give the word *wait* a bad name. But interestingly enough we have people with the title "waiters," and they are anything but snoozers. They are actively checking on people and serving them. Waiting is an action. It's not just sitting on the sidelines. The Thessalonians were busy serving while they waited for Christ's return. As Christ-followers, we're not just standing by in some lobby waiting for God to call our number so we can get to heaven. We have things to do while He has us here!

Underline the entire verse 10 and draw a king's crown off to the side. We will use this symbol several times as we read through 1 Thessalonians. Why? Because Paul reminded the Thessalonians often that Jesus was coming back. I chose the crown image to symbolize the return of our King Jesus. The Thessalonians actively waited in expectation for Jesus to return. Every morning they woke up and believed it could be the day they saw Christ face-to-face.

How do you think that impacted the way they served?

How do you think that impacted the culture they lived in?

The anticipation of this reality is central to our faith in Christ! Unfortunately, many Christians today have let little expectations block the big expectation that we should be focused on. Friends, is it possible that we are wasting time on things that have little eternal significance, when we should be waiting with expectation for the Faithful One who most certainly will return?

In the space below, make a list of the things you tend to wait expectantly for on the left-hand side. On the right-hand side make a list of how those things could become idols or false gods.

Things you wait expectantly for	How these things could become idols

The Thessalonian believers ditched their idols for the one true God! They had been waiting for these old non-living idols to fulfill their dreams but when they experienced the power of Christ, they knew the difference between death and life. They woke up! They turned, served, and learned to wait patiently on God. And so should we.

SHARE YOUR STORY

Challenge: *What would it look like to wake up every morning living as if it is the day you will meet Jesus face-to-face? Share how you would live if today is the day.*

#FaithfulOne

SESSION 2

Filled with Faith

1 THESSALONIANS 2:1-20

1 For you yourselves know, brothers, that our visit with you was not without result. 2 On the contrary, after we had previously suffered, and we were treated outrageously in Philippi, as you know, we were emboldened by our God to speak the gospel of God to you in spite of great opposition. 3 For our exhortation didn't come from error or impurity or an intent to deceive. 4 Instead, just as we have been approved by God to be entrusted with the gospel, so we speak, not to please men, but rather God, who examines our hearts. 5 For we never used flattering speech, as you know, or had greedy motives—God is our witness— 6 and we didn't seek glory from people, either from you or from others. 7 Although we could have been a burden as Christ's apostles, instead we were gentle among you, as a nursing mother nurtures her own children. 8 We cared so much for you that we were pleased to share with you not only the gospel of God but also our own lives, because you had become dear to us. 9 For you remember our labor and hardship, brothers. Working night and day so that we would not burden any of you, we preached God's gospel to you. 10 You are witnesses, and so is God, of how devoutly, righteously, and blamelessly we conducted ourselves with you believers. 11 As you know, like a father with his own children, 12 we encouraged, comforted, and implored each one of you to walk worthy of God, who calls you into His own kingdom and glory. 13 This is why we constantly thank God, because when you received the message about God that you heard from us, you welcomed it not as a human message, but as it truly is, the message of God, which also works effectively in you believers. 14 For you, brothers, became imitators of God's churches in Christ Jesus that are in Judea, since you have also suffered the same things from people of your own country, just as they did from the Jews 15 who killed both the Lord Jesus and the prophets and persecuted us; they displease God and are hostile to everyone, 16 hindering us from speaking to the Gentiles so that they may be saved. As a result, they are always completing the number of their sins, and wrath has overtaken them at last. 17 But as for us, brothers, after we were forced to leave you for a short time (in person, not in heart), we greatly desired and made every effort to return and see you face to face. 18 So we wanted to come to you—even I, Paul, time and again—but Satan hindered us. 19 For who is our hope or joy or crown of boasting in the presence of our Lord Jesus at His coming? Is it not you? 20 For you are our glory and joy!

Remember when you were little and you went to birthday parties with games like "Pin the Tail on the Donkey" or the dangling piñata of mysterious goodness? The piñata should never have been allowed at a kid's birthday party if you ask me. You give a little kid a stick, and you're already asking for trouble. But give them a stick AND blindfold them? I'm not very good at math, but that's an equation I know will end badly.

It doesn't take long for children of any age to figure out that the objective is to break open that piñata. For kids, the motivation to knock a hole into the mysterious paper-mache masterpiece is quite simple: getting to the treasure inside!

If you could design the perfect piñata, what would it look like? And more importantly, what would it hold inside? Draw it in the space below.

Now, imagine you step up to hit the above piñata, you feel the stick make contact, and you bust a hole in the side! But nothing comes out. So you swing again. Still nothing. Then you hear the murmurs. You take your blindfold off and discover for yourself that it is...(GASP) empty! An empty piñata! That's the worst, right? There is supposed to be a prize inside!

Can you think of other objects that can appear from the outside to be full of something, but often prove to be empty?

A few things that may have come to mind:
+ a chocolate bunny that's hollow
+ a piggy bank that rattles but contains only pennies
+ a fancy purse with nothing inside

Using that imagery, let's consider some spiritual implications.

Is it possible for Christians to share the good news of Christ with motives that are empty of Christ's love?

What could be some empty motives?

Is it possible for Christians to appear like empty piñatas to a desperate and hurting world around us? If so, explain.

We must be careful not to merely claim Christ as our hope when life is good, then fall to pieces when difficult circumstances hit. People want to know our hope is real and that the message we proclaim is filled with genuine faith in the One we claim as Lord and Savior.

Between the Lines

As we dig into 1 Thessalonians chapter 2, I want you to continue interacting with the text. Use the Scripture page for each session (p. 23 for Session Two) to underline, circle, and draw symbols as we study.

Read chapter 2 together. From the very beginning of this chapter, we discover a shift in the tone and content of the letter. Here, Paul addressed accusations about himself and about the message he proclaimed at Thessalonica. He had heard that those who were instrumental in running him out of town had openly questioned his motives. The ultimate goal of their accusations was to deter the new Thessalonian believers in their faith.

Underline without result in verse 1. The original Greek is *kenos* which means empty or hollow. **Now, circle the word *not* in that same verse.**

The message that Paul and his companions had preached was the work of Christ—the death of Christ on the cross and His resurrection. He knew that message had taken root which meant their visit was *not* "without result" or "empty" as it pertained to the Thessalonians. Paul spoke later to the church at Corinth about something similar. He said in 1 Corinthians 15:14, *"And if Christ has not been raised, then our preaching is in vain and your faith is in vain"* (ESV). The word *vain* comes from the same Greek word *kenos*, and means empty or hollow.

Paul was not like the traveling evangelists who came through town spouting off words in order to make money. He was preaching the work of Christ. If Paul emptied his proclamation of Christ and proclaimed anything else as the gospel, then their faith would have been based on a worthless message.

WORD STUDY

Kenos: Greek word for *without result*; some translations use the phrase *in vain* to denote the same idea. Kenos means empty or hollow.[8]

CROSS REFERENCE

Paul had a similar message for the Corinthians as he did in I Thessalonians 2:1 pertaining to the validity of the message they proclaimed. Paul's words in I Corinthians 15:14 used the same Greek word, *kenos*, for *vain*. Some translations say *without result* but it is the same concept.

CROSS REFERENCE

At the beginning of chapter 2, we see Paul's concern for the Thessalonians to embrace the message of Christ's work as the foundation of their faith. He referred to this again in chapter 3, verse 5 when he said, *I sent [Timothy] to learn about your faith, for fear that somehow the tempter had tempted you and our labor would be in vain* (ESV).

It would not have been good news at all. They would have been deceived by words that promised one thing but in the end were empty of the power to save.[9]

Without Christ's death and resurrection, there is no salvation. That's why any spiritual message not built on this reality is empty and lifeless. Preachers and teachers throughout history have garnered large followings by simply manipulating the message. Any message that leaves out the work of Christ on behalf of sinners is nothing more than a spiritual pep talk to make us feel better in the moment, but leaves us empty for eternity.

Have you heard messages that seemed like good news, but left out the work of Christ as the foundation? Share some examples.

What happens when people place their faith in an empty message like this?

How is that like the piñata we discussed earlier?

Paul wanted to make sure that the Thessalonians had truly put their faith in a Christ-filled message and not something empty. As we move through chapter two, we can almost picture Paul as a lawyer defending his case in court. He offered evidence of the validity of the gospel as well as their pure motives for sharing that message with the Thessalonians.

What evidence did Paul submit in verses 3-4 regarding their motives?

What were some ways that Paul, Timothy, and Silas lived while with the Thessalonians that reinforced that their motivation was Christ and not something else?

Who were they trying to please? (v. 4)

What did they not seek? (v. 6)

What else did they share with the Thessalonians besides the message of Christ? (v. 8)

Who else got called to the witness stand? (v. 10)

Underline <u>You are witnesses, and so is God</u> and draw a courtroom gavel in the margin to remind us that our lives should be evidence of the message we proclaim.

Reflect and Respond

Paul, Timothy, and Silas were willing to have their lives and motives examined regarding the work of Christ in and through them.

What about you? What is your faith based on?

What evidence is there that the message you proclaim and the life you live match up?

SHARE YOUR STORY

Challenge: *What message do you want your life to proclaim to the world?*

#FaithfulOne

Before you get started, make sure you are in a place free from distractions and ready to dig into God's Word. Remember to turn off your devices or switch them to "do not disturb" so you can give Him all your attention. Begin this time with prayer to focus your heart.

As we dig into 1 Thessalonians chapter 2, I want you to continue interacting with the text. Use page 23 to underline, circle, and draw as we dig deeper into this passage.

Read chapter 2 again. As you read, underline phrases that catch your attention. Feel free to write out questions you may have as you read.

Look back at verse 4 and underline the word please. Draw a conversation bubble above the word with the phrase, "LIKE ME" written in it.

Paul's purpose for sharing the gospel with the Thessalonians was not to gain their favor. He shared the message of Christ with them because that was what God called him to do. Although the circumstances are vastly different in our culture today, we can relate to this idea of trying to please people and gain their favor. We have a whole mode of communication called social media geared towards this.

What are some examples of how people seek approval through social media channels?

Have you ever tailored your "message" in order to gain more "likes" or "retweets"?

Have you ever backed down from something you believed in or took a different stance in order to gain popularity with a particular group of people? Explain.

How would your words and actions be different if you lived to please God and not man?

Paul and his friends encountered this as they preached in the synagogue at Thessalonica. The synagogue itself had drawn a mob of people, including government officials, who gathered to persecute Christians. Paul could have made a decision to cater to the people who were influential in the area in order to stay in the city. However, that was not what he had been called to do.

Paul and his companions remained faithful to God and to the gospel message no matter the cost. **Underline the word <u>examines</u> in verse 4 and draw a magnifying glass in the margin.** According to this verse, God looks intently at the heart. He can identify even better than we can the motives of our hearts. Sometimes the words we say may seem like they are pleasing to God, but in our hearts we are really saying them to gain the approval or praise of others.

Verse 6 specifies that Paul did not seek "glory" or "praise" from people. The fact that he makes this statement indicates that we, as human beings, are drawn to the praise of others. Hear me when I say that desiring encouragement and kind words is not wrong. We all need affirmation. But when we begin to base our identity, significance, and purpose on those words, we will find ourselves restless and empty. Living to please God and glorify His name is the life we were created for! He speaks words of truth and affirmation to our hearts that nothing else can compare to.

How healthy is your heart right now? Is it feeding off the praise of others or thirsting for the presence of God?

We must seek our value in Christ alone and trust His Word for affirmation. Below are statements that remind us of who we are in Him. Circle the one(s) that you need to be reminded of today.

- **Romans 8:2**—I am set free from sin.
- **1 Corinthians 6:20**—I am not my own. I was bought with a price.
- **2 Corinthians 5:17**—I am a new creation.
- **Galatians 2:19**—I am crucified with Christ.
- **Ephesians 1:5**—I am adopted as His child.
- **Ephesians 2:10**—I am God's creation, created in Christ Jesus to do good works.
- **Ephesians 2:19**—I am a fellow citizen with God's people and a member of God's household.
- **Ephesians 2:22**—I am a dwelling place in which God lives.
- **Ephesians 3:12**—I am able to approach God with freedom and confidence.

When we know who we are in Christ, we are better equipped to take His message of hope to the world around us. When we are confident in His love for us, we pattern our lives to please Him instead of chasing after the attention and affection of people.

SHARE YOUR STORY

Challenge: *Encourage someone else with these truths today. Share one or more of the statements/verses above as a way of pointing others to God, who is the source of your hope and security.*

#FaithfulOne

Begin this time with prayer to focus your heart and invite God to make you alert to whatever He wants to teach you today. Continue using page 23 to underline, circle, and draw as we dig deeper into chapter two.

Read the chapter and circle any words or phrases that stick out to you this time through.

Underline the words, _mother_ and _children_ in verse 7. Draw a picture of a pacifier near these words. This imagery of being nurtured is something we all long for and can relate to on some level.

Think back to your childhood. What memories can you recall when your mother or someone close to you was particularly nurturing to you?

There is a special kind of gentleness typically associated with the care of children. This is the imagery Paul wanted the Thessalonians to picture when they remembered the way he and his companions cared for them while they were in Thessalonica. The Thessalonians were new believers, infants in their faith, and Paul nurtured them to help them grow. So often with new Christians, we celebrate the beginning of their faith journey but lose sight of the discipleship process that must happen for them to "grow up" in their faith.

What are some intentional ways we as Christ-followers could nurture and care for friends that have just received Christ as Savior?

Paul used maternal and paternal imagery in this passage to associate the way they cared for the Thessalonians as more than just friends. They were family. The relationship I had with my father as I grew up was a difficult one. Thankfully as I journeyed with my church family, God was faithful to bring other "father figures" into my life to help support me and tell me that they were proud of me. As the Thessalonians experienced persecution, some may have even lost immediate family members. The church was supposed to come alongside them and embrace them as family.

Go back through chapter 2 and put a box around every reference to a family member like brother, sister, mother, or father. Make your box look like a picture frame to represent this concept of family the Thessalonians were discovering. Just like God provided family for the believers in Thessalonica, God is faithful to unite us with a church family today. We are called to love each other as brothers and sisters in Christ. We are called to be involved in each other's lives like family. Paul exhibited this process as he went from being a stranger in Thessalonica to a part of the family in a short span of time.

Many of us have family photos on our walls at home, but we don't often get the opportunity to celebrate our church family in pictures. Below is a drawing of a picture frame. As you think through how God has brought people from the church into your life, draw stick figures with corresponding initials to denote who each person is in your family of faith—a brother, sister, mother figure, or father figure in your life.

Take a moment now and give thanks to God for His faithfulness in providing these nurturing influences in your faith walk.

All throughout Scripture, we find references to being children of God and reminders that we are brothers and sisters in Christ. We are called to love each other with the love of Christ. Maybe you have been having a hard time with a member of your faith family. Begin today to pray that God will bring healing and increase your love for one another. If there are issues that need to be addressed, go to that person in a spirit of gracious humility and express your desire to be reconciled in your relationship. God is faithful and capable to help you to love one another like family.

SHARE YOUR STORY

Challenge: *Write out a statement that communicates why we are to love one another as the family of God.*

#FaithfulOne

Pause and pray before you get started. Continue using page 23 to underline, circle, and draw as we dig deeper into the passage.

At the beginning of this study, we talked about ways of sending and receiving messages. Paul mentioned the word *message* several times in verse 13. **Underline this word, then draw a small envelope in the margin to call attention to the importance of the message. Now, circle the word *thank* in verse 13 and place the turkey symbol in the margin.**

Paul thanked God because his friends received the message and submitted their lives to Christ. Take a moment and remember your own salvation experience. Think about the following:

✦ Where were you when you heard about the good news of Jesus Christ?

✦ Who shared the message of salvation with you and helped you understand God's love?

✦ Who was the first person you shared the news with after becoming a Christian?

We should constantly thank God for our own salvation and for the salvation of those we know. The message of redemption should overflow into our words and actions. There is nothing more important in life than receiving and sharing the gospel.

Read verse 9. Underline the word <u>labor</u> and draw a picture in the margin to symbolize a tent. Why are you drawing a tent? A cross reference to this verse is Acts 18:3. Read this and discover what Paul did to make a living while preaching in places like Thessalonica.[10] It was not uncommon for traveling philosophers in Paul's day to come through town and share their message in exchange for money. Paul wanted to make sure there was no confusion about his motivation for sharing the gospel of Jesus Christ.

When have you shared the hope of the gospel with friends, family, or acquaintances?

Did you experience any obstacles or resistance when you shared that message? Explain.

If you have experienced the joy of getting to see someone come to faith in Christ, write his or her name or initials here.

If you were able to write the names or initials of people you've seen come to a saving faith in Christ, take some time to thank God for the kingdom work you got to participate in. Thank Him for their faith! If there is someone you have been sharing with that is resistant to the gospel—keep praying. Keep being faithful to do whatever it takes to share and live out the message of grace.

My grandmother recently passed away at 96 years old. I remember as a little girl my mother sharing with my brother and I that our grandmother was not a believer. From that time on, we talked about Jesus whenever we were with her. We prayed for her regularly. I won't lie, there were times when I thought her heart was too hardened by sin and it was too late for her to ever change. I knew that God could do anything, yet I wondered if He would save my grandma at such an old age when she had spent her life rebelling against Him. But God continued to pursue her heart. Even in her nursing home, there was a believer that joined my mom in praying for grandma's salvation. The last week of her life, a minister from my home church joined my mom in sharing the plan of salvation with her again in the hospital room. This time, they were in for a huge surprise when my grandma exclaimed that a man (Jesus) had come to her while she was sleeping and she asked Him into her heart. She prayed to receive Christ because the Lord chose to reveal Himself to her in a dream. Before that night, she had been experiencing scary visions. We had been asking God to meet her any way possible. We believe that she had been seeing glimpses of the reality of being separated from God, and in her last days, she experienced the peace of His presence. My grandma for the first time in her life, *wanted* to pray with people. She raised her hands in celebration of "asking that man" to save her. Even in her last days, God made a way for her to come to a saving knowledge of Christ. I wondered why God would wait that long to save my grandma, but now I know. It's because He gets all the glory for it. I am forever grateful for the work of Christ in her heart.

It's a powerful reminder to me now as I sometimes grow tired from sharing the good news with those who seem resistant to His grace. I am called to be faithful to share as many times as God opens the door—it's not up to me to determine if someone has heard it enough…or if they are too old…or if they are too "far gone." My calling is to be faithful with the message of salvation.

Who has God placed in your life who needs to know about Christ? Begin praying for him or her today, that God will give you opportunities to proclaim His love to that person.

SHARE YOUR STORY

Challenge: *Share your testimony with the world of how Christ has saved you.*

#FaithfulOne

Before you get started, make sure you are in a place free from distractions and are ready to dig into God's Word. Continue using page 23 to underline, circle, and draw as we dig deeper into the passage. **Read all the way through chapter 2 again making note of anything that stands out to you as you read with fresh eyes.**

Underline the word <u>walk</u> in verse 12 and draw a footprint in the margin. We used a footprint in our study last week so it should bring back some thoughts from chapter one. This will be a common theme as Paul addresses the faith walk these new believers are on.

In that same verse, circle the word *kingdom*. Draw a simple castle in the margin of this verse. Paul used many types of pictures as he shared with the Thessalonians. One of the images he wanted them to think about often was the kingdom of God. He wanted them to know that as Christ-followers, they were living in someone else's earthly kingdom or empire, but they were always to live as citizens of God's kingdom.

Have you ever traveled outside of the country? If so, what places have you traveled to?

Describe the process of going through customs. What did you have to present and what are some of the questions they asked you?

When you were visiting these other places did anyone ever ask where you were from? Why do you think they asked?

It's usually pretty easy to tell a tourist from a native citizen. There are things we do that give clues to our citizenship. It could be the clothes we wear, the language we speak, or even the way we carry ourselves.

As Christ-followers, Paul wanted the Thessalonians to consider this reality—their faith and the manner in which they lived should indicate their Kingdom citizenship. The same is true for us. Although the Thessalonians were rightly concerned with the future and Christ's second coming, Paul wanted them to realize the present reality of living in the here and now.

Let's travel to other places in Scripture that talk about our citizenship as Christ-followers:
+ Philippians 3:20
+ 2 Corinthians 5:20
+ 1 Peter 2:11

What did you learn about our citizenship as Christ-followers?

We are set apart. There should be something different about the way we order our steps as God's people. If we are truly following Christ, then His footprints are leading us in a different direction than the world is going. But it is not our behavior that gives us access to God's kingdom. Just because I may go to church every Sunday and Wednesday does not make me a Christ-follower. It's like having someone from another country think that because they sing "The Star Spangled Banner" and celebrate the 4th of July, they are American. There is more to it than simply acting like a citizen.

What are examples of actions some might believe can gain them access to God's kingdom?

We don't obtain citizenship to God's kingdom by behaving like a Christian. Romans 10:9 tells us how salvation happens: *If you confess with your mouth, 'Jesus is Lord,' and believe in your heart that God raised Him from the dead, you will be saved.* We become citizens of God's kingdom when we recognize our desperate need for Jesus as Lord and Savior and respond by faith to His gracious invitation. Once we have that citizenship through salvation, the way we live and the paths we walk should testify to the fact that we have been transformed.

If you claim citizenship in God's kingdom, how does that affect the way you live?

SHARE YOUR STORY

Challenge: *Post a statement that clearly identifies your allegiance to Christ as Savior and Lord.*

#FaithfulOne

This is the last time you will read through chapter 2 this week. I'm so proud of your commitment to come and sit before God and learn from Paul's letter to the Thessalonians. Continue using page 23 to underline, circle, and draw symbols as you interact with the text.

Today we're going to focus on the last few verses of this chapter. Verse 17 always makes me think of a climactic part of a movie—the moment when the villain looks like he is triumphant by creating a wedge between friends or wreaking havoc on the heroes in the story.

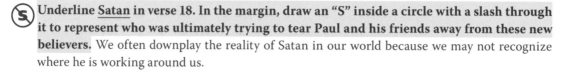

Underline the phrase, <u>forced to leave you</u> in verse 17. In the margin, draw a jagged line to represent the fact that Paul was torn away from the Thessalonians before he was ready to leave them. Though this seems at first glance like the schemes of the enemy have worked, think about this: because Paul and his companions were chased out of town so abruptly, God inspired Paul to follow-up by writing letters called 1 and 2 Thessalonians. God still gets the glory because so many Christ-followers have been able to receive the blessing of the truths found in these letters.

Underline <u>Satan</u> in verse 18. In the margin, draw an "S" inside a circle with a slash through it to represent who was ultimately trying to tear Paul and his friends away from these new believers. We often downplay the reality of Satan in our world because we may not recognize where he is working around us.

When I was younger, I took the following notes from a sermon and wrote them in the back of my Bible. I have never forgotten them, and they have been an encouragement to remind me that the fight is real. Satan desires to destroy the work of God's kingdom. I wrote down four D's that can be attributed to Satan's activity in this world:

+ Satan wants to **DEVOUR**. He is not playing around. He will try to devour reputations, marriages, families, finances, our time with God. What else have you seen him try to devour in your own life?

+ Satan wants to **DISCOURAGE**. He continually uses this one in particular to bring me down. And what happens when we're discouraged? We lose confidence. We become focused on ourselves and can't lift our heads to see others.

+ Satan wants to **DIVIDE.** I see this happen a lot in girls ministries. If Satan can divide, then he has weakened the impact of the whole team. The same is true for the church as a whole— if we are divided, then the work Jesus has called us to do is threatened.

+ Satan wants to **DIVERT.** This one is especially clever. His desire is to distract us and draw us away from the mission God has called us to. When this happens, the gospel gets pushed to the side as we pursue other things like success, relationships, money, etc.

Think about the enemy's tactics. How have you seen these exhibited in your own life or in the lives of those you love?

Ask God to give you the insight to recognize when Satan is using one of these tactics in your life.

Let's look back at today's passage. Notice the word that Paul used in 1 Thessalonians 2:18. Underline hindered. The word *hindered* implies that there's an immediate obstacle to be dealt with, but it doesn't mean the ultimate goal has been defeated. Paul knew God was still able to work even in the midst of spiritual warfare. Being in this battle can be discouraging at times, but ultimately we know that God wins! **Underline verse 19 and draw a king's crown in the margin** **as a reminder that Jesus is coming back!**

Read 1 Peter 5:8-11 from The Message translation.

✦ *Keep a cool head. Stay alert. The Devil is poised to pounce, and would like nothing better than to catch you napping. Keep your guard up. You're not the only ones plunged into these hard times. It's the same with Christians all over the world. So keep a firm grip on the faith. The suffering won't last forever. It won't be long before this generous God who has great plans for us in Christ—eternal and glorious plans they are!—will have you put together and on your feet for good. He gets the last word; yes, he does.*

Are you facing anything right now that is hindering you from pursuing Christ or sharing His message of hope? Explain.

Whenever I feel an intense spiritual battle raging around me, it helps to remember that Satan has already been defeated and Christ is the victor! Close in prayer, asking God to remind you to be on your guard against the four D's and to encourage you that He has already defeated the enemy.

SHARE YOUR STORY

Challenge: *In your own words, post a statement that highlights this reality: Victory belongs to our God.*

#FaithfulOne

SESSION 3

A Sturdy Foundation

1 THESSALONIANS 3:1-13

1 Therefore, when we could no longer stand it, we thought it was better to be left alone in Athens. 2 And we sent Timothy, our brother and God's coworker in the gospel of Christ, to strengthen and encourage you concerning your faith, 3 so that no one will be shaken by these persecutions. For you yourselves know that we are appointed to this. 4 In fact, when we were with you, we told you previously that we were going to suffer persecution, and as you know, it happened. 5 For this reason, when I could no longer stand it, I also sent him to find out about your faith, fearing that the tempter had tempted you and that our labor might be for nothing. 6 But now Timothy has come to us from you and brought us good news about your faith and love and reported that you always have good memories of us, wanting to see us, as we also want to see you. 7 Therefore, brothers, in all our distress and persecution, we were encouraged about you through your faith. 8 For now we live, if you stand firm in the Lord. 9 How can we thank God for you in return for all the joy we experience before our God because of you, 10 as we pray very earnestly night and day to see you face to face and to complete what is lacking in your faith? 11 Now may our God and Father Himself, and our Lord Jesus, direct our way to you. 12 And may the Lord cause you to increase and overflow with love for one another and for everyone, just as we also do for you. 13 May He make your hearts blameless in holiness before our God and Father at the coming of our Lord Jesus with all His saints. Amen.

If you are anything like me, then you enjoy an evening of board games with friends and family. One of my favorite games is Jenga®—you know, the one with the tower made of blocks where the objective is to take a block from the structure and place it on top without causing the whole thing to collapse. The anticipation of wondering if the tower will fall each time a piece is pulled out never fails to enthrall me. Maybe it's because I enjoy yelling "JENGA" when the tower falls. I'm not sure you are really supposed to do that, but I do it anyway. I did some research one day and found out that the term *jenga* is the Swahili equivalent of our English word *build*.[11] It's kind of funny when you think that all these years when the tower is falling, I've actually been yelling "BUILD"!

Environment is key during a game of Jenga. You definitely don't want to play this game on a shaky table. You need a sturdy foundation because as the tower gets taller, the structure gets more and more susceptible to destruction. Even a slight bump can bring it all collapsing down.

Now let's consider some spiritual application to this game of structure and strategy. Just like in Jenga, our spiritual environment and foundation are incredibly important.

Based on what you know about the Thessalonians so far, what were some environmental dangers that threatened to shake their faith?

What was the foundation that Paul had taught them to build their faith upon?

As we dig into chapter 3 of 1 Thessalonians this week, look for times when Paul was, in essence, yelling "BUILD" to encourage these new believers. He saw some shaky things happening and before they collapsed under pressure, he wanted to challenge them and build up their faith.

Between the Lines

As we dig into 1 Thessalonians chapter 3, I want you to continue interacting with the text. Use the Scripture page for this session to underline, circle, and draw as we dig deeper into the passage. (See p. 39.)

Read chapter 3 together. As you begin reading, you immediately get a sense for how dearly Paul loved these new believers. When we look at verses 1 and 5, we find a phrase repeated. Whenever there is a repeated phrase in Scripture, take notice. The first instance says, "when we could no longer stand it." Then Paul repeats that idea in verse 5 by saying, "when I could no longer stand it."

Underline the repeated phrase in both verses.

It's evident that their hearts were united in Christ and when the Thessalonians were hurting, Paul was hurting too. Paul knew the persecution they were facing and sensed how deeply they needed some encouragement. He sent Timothy with a mission to help build up the faith of the Thessalonians during these difficult days.

As a response to Timothy's report of how things were going, Paul sent this letter to the church in Thessalonica.

Circle the word *shaken* in verse 3. Paul used the Greek word *sainesthai* translated as *shaken*. The picture associated with this particular Greek word is that of a dog wagging its tail back and forth.[12] Paul was fearful that the Thessalonians were wavering in their faith because of the persecution they faced.

Circle the word *strengthen* in verse 2. The word used in the original Greek is *sterizo* which means "to fix something so that it stands upright and immovable."[13] The picture associated with this word is that of tying a tender plant (that cannot stand on its own) to a stable pole or stick so it can grow sturdy.[14]

Timothy was there to help them develop sturdier roots in their walk with Christ so they could stand on their own as persecution came against them.

Who are you "tied" to in an accountability-type relationship that helps stabilize your faith during shaky times?

WORD STUDY

Sainesthai: Greek word translated as *shaken*

WORD STUDY

Sterizo: Greek word translated as *strengthen*; means to fix something so that it stands upright and immovable

Is there someone you are investing in and encouraging to grow spiritually? Explain.

The Thessalonians needed someone more mature in their faith to help them understand some basics about what it was they were waiting for and what they were to do in the waiting. In the midst of all their questions about the future, there were also people trying to discredit Paul and cause more confusion among these new believers.[15]

I am so thankful in my walk with Christ that He provides us with a community of spiritual brothers and sisters to walk alongside us on this journey. We can encourage one another with Scripture, through prayer, and by pointing out how we see God at work in each others' lives. We need people to cheer us on and remind us to build our faith on a sturdy foundation.

Reflect and Respond

Sometimes in our faith walk, we are so blinded by the circumstances that we can't see the big picture of where Christ is working in our lives. That's why it's so important to be in community with other believers.

Who are the people you are doing life with on a regular basis?

How have they encouraged and challenged you spiritually?

In what ways are you encouraging and challenging them spiritually?

Look around the room at the people you are participating in this study with. You are united in heart with your sisters in Christ. When they are hurting, you are called to encourage them. When they are growing, you are called to celebrate with them. Take some time to share with one another how things are going in life right now. Use the space provided to make notes of how you can pray for and encourage each other this week.

SHARE YOUR STORY

Challenge: *Share one reason why you are thankful for those who are walking alongside you spiritually.*

#FaithfulOne

Before you get started, make sure you are in a place free from distractions and ready to dig into God's Word. Remember to turn off your devices or switch them to "do not disturb" so you can give Him all your attention. Begin with a time of prayer to focus your heart on God. Invite Him to make you alert to whatever He desires to teach you through His Word.

As we dig into 1 Thessalonians chapter 3, I want you to continue interacting with the text. Use page 39 to underline, circle, and draw symbols as we dig deeper into this passage.

Read through the chapter and underline any statements or words that catch your attention. In addition, if you see themes from previous chapters, it may be helpful to make a note in the margin so you can see how Paul reinforces those messages.

Today we will address the absence of one of those messages. Sometimes you can draw conclusions about a passage by what isn't there just as much as by what is there. One of the styles that we have seen Paul use is writing in sets of three.

Do you remember the three attributes he used to describe the Thessalonians in chapter 1 verse 3? Their _____, _____, and _____. Feel free to look back in your book if you need to.

With those words in mind, read Timothy's report in chapter 3, verse 6. Paul mentioned what two things? _____ and _____.

Go back through the chapter and circle *faith* and *love* every time you see those words.

Draw the symbol we have been using for the word hope in the space below.

Timothy didn't report on their *hope*. Hope appears to be wavering for our friends, the Thessalonians. We will see Paul bring hope back into the picture in chapter four when he talks about grieving with hope.

Hope is a word we tend to toss around in everyday conversations, but we probably don't think very often about how valuable it is to our everyday lives.

How do we use the word *hope* in everyday conversations?

We sometimes use hope as more of a "wish list" kind of word—I hope I pass that test; I hope it doesn't rain today; I hope I make the team. And so on. The hope that the Thessalonians were wavering in was not a wishful thinking kind of hope. Wishful thinking leaves the outcome to chance. Real hope (the kind that lasts) leaves the outcome in God's hands. Spiritual hope comes from anchoring our lives and futures in God.

In verse 10, Paul said he prayed for them night and day. What was his prayer?

Paul desperately wanted the Thessalonians to experience the fullness of their faith. He wanted them to embrace hope even as they faced difficult times. Now it makes sense why Paul repeated the theme of Christ's return over and over again. His desire was to "complete what [was] lacking in [their] faith." In the midst of persecution, they needed to recognize that Jesus wasn't just their hope for eternity—He was also the hope that would sustain them on their darkest days.

SHARE YOUR STORY

Challenge: *Share a message of hope by completing this sentence: My hope is found...*

#FaithfuLOne

Pause and pray before you begin. Remember to use page 39 to underline, circle, and draw symbols as we dig deeper into the passage.

Let's approach today's reading a little differently. Consider reading through chapter 3 in a whisper. As you whisper, think about how the persecutors were trying to silence what God was doing in the lives of the Thessalonians.

Verse 2 tells us that Paul and Silas made a decision to send Timothy back to Thessalonica to check in with them. This would have been a dangerous mission for him to do by himself. Timothy was younger than Paul and Silas and was like a younger brother in ministry to them. He was less experienced at this point in his life, but he played a significant role in the discipleship process for the Thessalonians by carrying letters and news back and forth.

How is Timothy described in verse 2?
1.
2.

According to that same verse, what did Paul and Silas send Timothy to do?
1.
2.

▷ **Underline the word <u>coworker</u>. In the margin draw a small sports pennant and write GO TEAM on it.** Timothy and Paul were on the same team. They had the same mission and they served the same God. Timothy played a specific role on this ministry team as he followed Paul's leadership.

Have you ever served on a ministry or missions team?

What has been your role in those experiences?

What would happen if people on the team chose not to serve in the roles they were given? Who would be impacted?

Why is it important to function as a team when we are doing Kingdom work?

The apostle Paul had much to say throughout the New Testament about working together for the Kingdom. He gave instructions in several different passages to ensure that we as believers know how the church body is to function.

Read what Paul said in 1 Corinthians 12:4-6.
Now there are different gifts, but the same Spirit. There are different ministries, but the same Lord. And there are different activities, but the same God activates each gift in each person.

Verses 7-11 document examples of the gifts that we as Christians are given to use for Kingdom building. The picture that Paul gave us is a great example of teamwork. He finishes this section in verse 12 by saying, *For as the body is one and has many parts, and all the parts of that body, though many, are one body—so also is Christ.*

Timothy played his role in equipping the church at Thessalonians. Paul played his role. Silas played his. But they all were working together as Christ unified them with His Spirit and His purpose. Now, think about the role you play as part of your church.

What gifts has God given you and how are you using them to serve the church body?

How can you encourage the other people you serve alongside and be a cheerleader for them?

Every part of the team is significant, just like every part of the body is put together with a purpose. If there are areas where you are causing division instead of building up the body of Christ, ask a parent, mentor, or student ministry leader to help you work through issues.

SHARE YOUR STORY

Challenge: *Share some reasons you love your church.*

#FaithfulOne

Begin today by thanking God for what He has been teaching you through His Word. Continue using page 39 to interact with the text as you read.

 Read through chapter 3 now. Circle the word *persecution* every time you see it. In the margin, draw the symbol of the bandage which we used earlier in the study. For us to get the full impact of these verses, we need to understand that the persecution the Thessalonians experienced hit every part of their lives—from emotional to physical to spiritual. From across the miles, Paul and his companions suffered severe persecution as well.

According to verse 7, what brought Paul comfort during this difficult time?

Verse 9 talks about Paul's joy. What brought that joy?

Who did Paul thank for the faith and growth the Thessalonians were experiencing?

It is important to remember that while mentors and accountability partners are used by God to help us grow stronger in our walk, it is always Christ's work that transforms us. Paul did not try to take credit for the work he knew only God could do in the lives of the Thessalonians.

Recently in the student ministry where I serve, several students experienced an awakening (independently of each other) to the lostness of their school and friends. As a result, I received texts, direct messages, and Instagrams celebrating how Christ had used them to share their faith with friends. Even in the last week, I heard about two people coming to know Christ as Lord and Savior through the testimony of a middle school girl and several high schoolers. While these students were obedient to share their faith, *all* glory goes to God. Only He can transform lives.

Matthew 5:16 is one of my favorite verses. It says, *In the same way, let your light shine before men, so that they may see your good works and give glory to your Father in heaven.* We are called to let our light shine—not so people see us, but so they see the Faithful One inside us!

Christ is not just at work in our salvation. As we stay near Him, He continually grows and transforms us to be more like Him.

How have you seen Christ at work in your life lately?

Not only do we need to celebrate spiritual growth in our own lives, we should also be mindful of how God is working in others. When Paul heard about how Christ was at work in the Thessalonians, it encouraged him.

Why do you think hearing about Christ's work in their lives encouraged him?

When was the last time that you celebrated how Christ was at work in the life of friend or family member?

Earlier in this letter, Paul made mention of the Thessalonians being like a trophy when he said in 2:19 that they were like a *crown of boasting* before the Lord Jesus. It's not that Paul took credit for their faith, he was just boasting in the faithfulness of Christ who worked in and through him to reach the Thessalonians. We should also look for reasons to boast in the Lord. We should celebrate the ways He has used our gifts, talents, and passions to reveal Himself to the world around us. And we should make much of the work He is doing in the lives of those we know and love.

SHARE YOUR STORY

Challenge: *Boast in the Lord today. Share something He has done in or through you this week.*

#FaithfulOne

Pause and pray before you dig into today's study. Continue to use page 39 to underline, circle, and draw symbols that will help you remember the truths you are learning.

As you read chapter 3 again, look at the themes you have already noted in the margins. Think through how you see those themes showing up in your own life.

How have you seen God's faithfulness as you have been faithful to study His Word each day?

Have you ever been prayer walking? I never gave this much thought until I heard evidence of God at work through prayer walks in several countries I had the opportunity to visit. The places I visited all were less than one or two percent Christian. They were spiritually dark countries. When I would meet with Christians in these places, their *first* response to any obstacle was, "Have we prayed about this?"

As a result, I began adopting prayer walking as part of my normal routine. I have even done some drive-by praying. One of my favorite descriptions of prayer walking is "praying onsite with insight."[16] As you walk, you see actual faces, scenery and buildings. It's not unusual for the Lord to bring things to your heart that you need to pray for as you walk along. Sometimes the prayers are answered during the walk. Sometimes it's years before those prayers are answered. However, God's faithfulness is seen in amazing ways no matter how much time passes between the request and the outcome. One recent example—our church felt called to reach the lost in a different area of town from our main campus so we began looking for a new building. During a prayer walk, a person on our team saw the owner of a building place a "For Rent" sign out on the very spot where our new campus is launching. God answered that prayer and honored the faithfulness of those who sought His insight.

In another country where I help lead a group of students every summer, we heard stories about a man from the community who prayer walked up the mountain every Saturday for over 10 years. What was he praying for? He was praying for a church to be planted on that mountain. Every summer, we get to go and serve alongside members who belong to that answered prayer.

Paul understood the importance of prayer. Often as he was writing to the Thessalonians, he would stop and write a prayer for them. He did this because prayer is vital to the work we do as Christ-followers.

 Read verse 11-13. This is a prayer Paul is writing on behalf of the Thessalonians. Make a circle around this section, then draw a pair of praying hands in the margin.

What are the requests that Paul makes on behalf of his friends?

Verse 13 gives us insight into Paul's ultimate desire for them. His prayer was for their hearts to be made blameless and holy by the Lord's grace and strength. The Thessalonians were dealing with a lot in their community so Paul was praying for their hearts to be purified in the midst of it all.

As you close out today's study, let's really put feet to this idea. Pick a place in your community to prayer walk. I use the following as a guide for my prayer walking time and think it might be helpful to you.

How do you pray?

+ **Pray with discernment**—Pray for Christ to give you His eyes and heart for the area you are praying for. How is He already at work? What do you notice about the needs of the community?
+ **Pray for blessing**—Pray over every person, home, and business you encounter; for God's intervention in each life, so that each one can be fruitful in God's kingdom; for God's will to be done in this community.
+ **Pray with compassion**—Try and walk in the shoes of those you encounter. See and feel what residents live with every day; offer intercession for those things that express brokenness and grieve God's spirit; give thanks to God for the blessings and gifts that exist in the community.
+ **Pray from Scripture**—Prayers based directly on God's Word can be especially powerful. You may want to bring a Bible with key passages highlighted, or copy verses onto note cards.
+ **Pray in God's power**—allow times of silence for God's Spirit to speak to you or through you (Rom. 8:26). Ask with confidence in the power of Jesus' name (John 14:12-14). Like the disciples sent out by Christ, we are empowered to push back the darkness (Luke 10:17-18).

SHARE YOUR STORY

Challenge: *Share some thoughts from your prayer walking experience.*

#FaithfulOne

I really am proud of how you have stuck with this. I'm sure that in the midst of all the craziness of life, you have had to fight for this time with the Lord. Keep fighting! It's so worth it! As you read chapter 3 again this week, let it pour over you. Soak it in. Look back over your questions, themes, and drawings on page 39. Keep using this page to record what you are learning.

Is there anything that God has awakened within your heart or perhaps brought a magnifying glass to during this particular week of study? Explain.

Let's dive in and take a look at the last key verse we're going to study in chapter 3. Yesterday, we looked at the prayer Paul prayed for the Thessalonians. I want to zoom in and focus on one section of that prayer today. **Read verse 12 and underline the words increase and overflow. Off to the side of these words, draw a heart with the "greater than" symbol after it.** So in essence, the symbol should make you think love more and more.

❤ >

Paul wanted the Thessalonians to love more and more. He wanted to see them increase and overflow with love.

Who does Paul tell them to love?
1.
2.

It's easy to figure out who the "one another" are. They are the Thessalonian believers. So who fits in the other category of "everyone"? Really think about that one. When Paul calls them to love everyone, he is actually calling them to love even those who are persecuting them.

Have you ever had a "mean girl" or bully in your life?

I had someone who picked on me from middle school to around my sophomore year of high school. I will never forget the day I finally got my first pair of trendy, name brand jeans. I was so excited until she found a way to shame me. She waited until a lot of people were out in the hallway between the busiest hour, and yelled: "Is that the only pair of Guess jeans you have, Amy-Jo?" It was all we could afford, and if I'm truly being honest, I knew my mom made some significant sacrifices just to buy that one pair.

I have story after story of this bully. It doesn't sound as bad as some of you have it, but over and over again she would strike when I least expected it. She delighted in publicly humiliating me. Eventually the story changed in my favor. I discovered her real name one day when her father ran into me. She was horrified and was always worried I might use it against her publicly. Instead of wielding that power, I decided to turn things around on her. I began to help her with her Spanish homework. I helped her out when she needed something that I could give. I heaped love on her with words and actions. It was one of the hardest things I tried to do. Even in a small way, this experience helped me more fully understand what it means to love "everyone," even when it includes those who are hard to love.

Paul was calling the Thessalonians to not only love those in the church but also those who were persecuting the church...their enemies.

Without naming names—is there someone right now that you are having a hard time loving?

The word choices that Paul used, *increase* and *overflow* make me think of a fountain. It grows and overflows. That picture of love for the person you mentioned above seems impossible doesn't it? That's because it is impossible. Unless you look closer at how that love was grown in the Thessalonians.

Who it is that makes our love increase and overflow?

Only Christ at work within us can make a fountain out of a desert. As you close out today, spend some time in prayer inviting Christ to help you to love the people in your family, your church, your community, and even the people who are your enemies. Share with Jesus about the wounds that are in your heart. Ask Him to help you forgive those who have hurt you. He understands that pain more than you know. After all, He forgave us. Let Him show you His faithfulness in the most painful places in your heart. (NOTE: If you are experiencing wounds that are physical or emotional, please love yourself enough to tell an adult about the circumstances this very day.)

SHARE YOUR STORY

Challenge: *Memorize 1 Thessalonians 3:12 and post it on social media as a reminder to love deeply.*

#FaithfulOne

Connected to Christ

1 THESSALONIANS 4:1-18

1 Finally then, brothers, we ask and encourage you in the Lord Jesus, that as you have received from us how you must walk and please God—as you are doing—do so even more. 2 For you know what commands we gave you through the Lord Jesus. 3 For this is God's will, your sanctification: that you abstain from sexual immorality, 4 so that each of you knows how to control his own body in sanctification and honor, 5 not with lustful desires, like the Gentiles who don't know God. 6 This means one must not transgress against and defraud his brother in this matter, because the Lord is an avenger of all these offenses, as we also previously told and warned you. 7 For God has not called us to impurity but to sanctification. 8 Therefore, the person who rejects this does not reject man, but God, who also gives you His Holy Spirit. 9 About brotherly love: You don't need me to write you because you yourselves are taught by God to love one another. 10 In fact, you are doing this toward all the brothers in the entire region of Macedonia. But we encourage you, brothers, to do so even more, 11 to seek to lead a quiet life, to mind your own business, and to work with your own hands, as we commanded you, 12 so that you may walk properly in the presence of outsiders and not be dependent on anyone. 13 We do not want you to be uninformed, brothers, concerning those who are asleep, so that you will not grieve like the rest, who have no hope. 14 Since we believe that Jesus died and rose again, in the same way God will bring with Him those who have fallen asleep through Jesus. 15 For we say this to you by a revelation from the Lord: We who are still alive at the Lord's coming will certainly have no advantage over those who have fallen asleep. 16 For the Lord Himself will descend from heaven with a shout, with the archangel's voice, and with the trumpet of God, and the dead in Christ will rise first. 17 Then we who are still alive will be caught up together with them in the clouds to meet the Lord in the air and so we will always be with the Lord. 18 Therefore encourage one another with these words.

Do you remember those connect-the-dots activity sheets from childhood? I was always so enamored with what the mystery image would turn out to be. I couldn't wait to figure it out! I would start with number 1 and just keep sliding my crayon from number to number until the picture took shape.

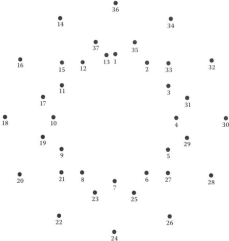

Okay, so you might be asking, what does a connect-the-dots picture have in common with the Thessalonians? I'm glad you asked. Look at you. You're already trying to connect the dots to this lesson. As we dig into chapter 4, we will discover several topics that Paul addressed with his friends. As I was reading through this, I wondered how all these topics related to one another. Or were they just a list of things that Paul felt he needed to cover before he closed out his letter?

Topics he focused on:
+ Sexual Purity
+ Relationships
+ Grieving
+ Death
+ Future

When you look at these topics, it appears to be a laundry list of complex issues that need to be dealt with separately. However, Paul used an ancient form of writing to address all these areas of concern with the Thessalonians. Paul instructed them with a "do this, not that" approach, trusting that they would live this out by the power of Christ at work within them. As Christ-followers, we don't live segmented lives. More bluntly...we don't leave Jesus at church and pick Him up when we return the following Sunday. The fact is, when the resurrected Christ enters our lives, He connects the dots in such a way that every aspect of our lives is impacted by Him.

Between the Lines

Use page 55 to underline, circle, and draw as we dig deeper into this passage.

Read chapter 4 together. The "laundry list" of items Paul goes over is segmented into the following verses. What are the key instructions in each section? Write them in the boxes below.

CULTURAL CONTEXT

Paul was relating to a culture that was not very literate. As a result, it required repetitive oral teaching.

Reference	Issue	Instructions
Verses 3-8	*Sexual Purity/Holiness*	
Verses 9-10	*Brotherly Love*	
Verses 11-12	*Community Love*	
Verses 13-15a	*Grieving with Hope*	
Verses 15b-18	*Christ's Return*	

The Thessalonians had received some of this instruction during Paul's first visit as he taught it orally and by example. They were very much like children in their ability to soak up all the actions that Paul, Silas, and Timothy modeled before them. All throughout this letter, you see echoes of what Paul was trying to reinforce through inviting them to copy his life as he copied the life of Christ.

Although you'll find instructions for these issues in other places in this letter (and other places in Scripture), without the resurrected Christ threaded through all of it, life just feels fragmented and chaotic. Our lives should be so connected to Christ that His grace defines how we view sex, how we grieve, how we love our family (both biological and church) and how we love our community.

Circle the word *walk* in verse 1 of chapter 4. *Peripatéō* is the Greek word translated walk or live. You'll find the phrase *how you must walk and please God* in this verse. These are not two separate thoughts. In the Greek, these two actions create one idea. The way we conduct our lives is an act of worship. It's connected together—unable to be separated.[17]

These spiritual connections to sex, grief, family, community, and future destiny were completely foreign to the Thessalonians until Paul shared the good news of Jesus Christ. The same is true in our culture today. Enjoying the gift of sex the way God designed it is an act of worship to God. Using the gift outside the parameters God has put in place is sinful and selfish.

How does God's design for sex demonstrate true love?

Now let's look at the rest of Paul's list.

How should the love of Christ in us transform the way we love other believers?

How should the way we live as Christ-followers impact our community?

How is it that we have hope, even in grief?

How does the return of the risen Christ impact our past, present, and future?

Reflect and Respond

Let's check out Paul's instructions in another letter addressed to the church in Galatia. Turn in your Bibles and read Galatians 5:16-26 together.

You see a thread of the same issues and instructions here as we did in chapter 4 of 1 Thessalonians.

In what areas of life are you trying to "walk" in your own power instead of leaning into the power of the Holy Spirit?

Pray a spirit of surrender in those areas where you have disconnected from Christ. Invite Him to fill those places with His grace so that you can live a life of worship, dedicated to Him alone.

SHARE YOUR STORY

Challenge: *Share how you have seen Christ work in any of the areas we focused on today (purity, church family, community, grief, hope for eternity).*

#FaithfulOne

Before you get started, make sure you are in a place free from distractions and ready to dig into God's Word. Remember to turn off your devices or switch them to "do not disturb" so you can give Him all your attention. Continue using page 55 to underline, circle, and draw symbols that will help you remember the truths you are learning.

Begin this time with prayer to focus your heart. Invite God to truly make you alert to whatever He has for you to learn, confess, or live out today.

As you read chapter 4 for the first time on your own, remember to underline the words and phrases that stick out to you. Write question marks or exclamation points off to the side of any verses you want to explore a little further.

Look for the phrase, <u>as you are doing—do so even more</u>. When you find it, underline it. Then draw a yard stick or ruler in the margin as a sign of measurement.

Paul wanted to see evidence of growth in the lives of the Thessalonians. The statement *even more* was a challenge for them to dig deeper and to never stop growing. And Paul knew that the only way for them to do this, was to cling even more to Christ.

Did you ever measure anything when you were growing up? If so, what?

What did you use to measure things with?

Parents often will have a height chart to show a child how much they have grown. Height is easy to measure with the right tool. It's harder to measure our love or our holiness, isn't it? Paul encouraged the Thessalonians by affirming that their love and holiness was evident. But he wanted them to keep growing. Why? Because spiritual growth means transformation, also known as *sanctification*. (We'll talk more about this word in our next session.)

According to verse 3, why should we desire sanctification?

Sanctification means that as Christ-followers we are set apart for God's purposes. The more we grow, the more set apart we become and the more we reflect God's glory to the world around us.

Read the following:
Mahatma Gandhi was India's revered leader in the fight for national independence from Britain. As a child in India, a student in England and a lawyer in South Africa, he was exposed to Christianity—and raw racism. He admired the teachings of Jesus, especially His Sermon on the Mount. He admired the life of Jesus and was inspired to follow His example. But after years of observing Christians he sadly concluded, 'For me to believe in their Redeemer, their lives must show they are redeemed.' He never became a Christian.[19]

How did the people that Gandhi observed and the Thessalonians differ in the way they lived?

Do you ever consider how much your words and actions influence the people around you? Why or why not?

How does the challenge, *as you are doing—do so even more*, impact your dependence on the Redeemer at work in you?

This week find someone you trust (a parent, mentor, close friend) and invite them to place a spiritual ruler against your life.
+ Ask them to help you see areas where you have grown.
+ Ask them to help you see areas that need to be developed.
+ Decide on one area that you would like to see God grow within you and pray for that area together.

SHARE YOUR STORY

Challenge: *Celebrate how the Lord has worked in your life so far during this study. Post one thing you have learned.*

#FaithfulOne

Pause and pray before you begin. Continue to use page 55 to interact with the text as we go through today's passage.

As you read through chapter 4, you'll come across the word <u>sanctification</u>**. Underline that word whenever you see it. In the margin, draw a white flag with a cross to symbolize surrender.**

The Greek word *hagiasmos* refers to the process of sanctification. The definition is: "set apart for God's special use, to make distinct from what is common, hence to be made like God who is distinct from all else and therefore holy. It is a process which is perfect but not yet attained."[20]

So, now in English please? As Christ-followers, Christ is at work within us continuing to make us more like Him. Once we are with Him in eternity, we will experience the full transformation of holiness.

The Thessalonians were dealing with a culture that had blurred all boundaries of purity and holiness. The Greek word Paul used for the phrase *sexual immorality*, is actually where we get our English word *pornography*. He was using a broad term to cover any ungodly sexual activity.

The following list may be offensive. I hope it is because it is offensive to God. These are issues that our culture deals with but these are not new to the human struggle. The Thessalonians were plagued with these temptations as well.

- **Sex outside of marriage**—which is adultery
- **Sex before marriage**—any act of sexual impurity
- **Sexual images**—pornography in a visual format or written format (e.g., Erotica novels)

These are issues Paul was very serious about. In fact, the translation of some of these verses is pretty graphic in what Paul was acknowledging as immoral.

Hebrews 10:10 says, *By this will of God, we have been sanctified through the offering of the body of Jesus Christ once and for all.*

What does this verse confirm about sanctification that we also learned in I Thessalonians 4:3?

Our bodies as Christ-followers are not our own. That's why I had you draw the white flag of surrender next to the word *sanctification*. It is a reminder that we have surrendered our bodies to be set apart for His use, for His glory...not for our selfish pleasure.

Have you ever seen one child take another child's toy? The word that came next never had to be taught. Any guesses what that word is? Mine. We may grow up and use more elaborate words, but at the heart of our selfishness, we shout out "MINE!" to God over areas that He is trying to pry out of our hands for His purposes. We think things like this: God gave us sex as a gift right? So it's OK to label it as mine! Not so fast. Turn in your Bible to Ephesians 5:25-32 and read this passage. Sex is a gift from God for a purpose.

To help illustrate this, draw a stick figure girl in the space provided. Next draw a stick figure guy. Now draw a heart around them. Now draw a cross between them.

How does knowing your heart and body belong to Christ impact the way you look at your sexuality?

God gave us sex to be enjoyed within the marriage relationship. It enhances the intimacy and draws a husband and wife together in a mysterious way. Scripture uses that same picture of intimacy in marriage to illustrate the relationship between Christ and the church. It's no wonder that Satan wants to destroy the purity of marriage. He wants to destroy anything that gives glory to Christ and His Bride.

Just like a framed wedding photo has boundaries, so does God's design for sex because it is set apart to bring glory to Him. Paul had to go into a culture where sex had no boundaries, remove all the labels that said "Mine" and replace them with labels that said "His." We must do the same in our own lives. Even if you have made mistakes in the area of sexual purity, you can experience God's beautiful grace and invite Him to switch the labels on your life from "Mine" to "His." Spend some time with Him today, wrestling with these tough issues.

SHARE YOUR STORY

Challenge: *Post 1 Thessalonians 4:7 as a statement of your desire to be sanctified and pleasing to God.*

#FaithfulOne

Begin this time with prayer. Ask God to open the eyes of your heart to the truths He wants to show you. Continue using page 55 to interact with the text as we underline, circle, and draw.

Today as we dig into another portion of chapter 4, we will see more evidence of how well the Thessalonians were expressing love. Remember in chapter 3, verse 12, Paul prayed this over them, *And may the Lord cause you to increase and overflow with love for one another and for everyone.* In the very next chapter we see Paul go back and point to specific examples of how they were increasing in love for one another and for those outside the faith.

❤ > **Read verses 9-12. Circle the words,** *one another* **and** *outsiders* **when you find them. Now, to serve as a reminder of the theme this is echoing from chapter 3, draw a heart with the "greater than" symbol after it.** Here Paul highlighted specific examples of how an ever increasing love was being exemplified in their everyday lives.

According to verse 9, who was teaching the Thessalonians how to love their "brothers"?

Isn't that cool?! God was at work in their hearts, prompting them to love in certain ways. They were learning new ways to love each other directly from the Author of love! It makes sense, after all, since the Bible tells us that God is love. Who better to teach a class on it than the Founder of love Himself?!

In verse 9, the word *brothers* is definitely a word that was used in the context of family. However, it became common for Christ-followers to extend the family role titles to those within the church body who were not blood relatives. It was an expression of love that reminded believers they were all connected through Christ.

What are some ways God has prompted you to express love to other Christians?

How have other believers in your church expressed love to you?

Let's move to verses 11-12. Underline the instructions Paul gave them for how to love and live among *outsiders* (this would be anyone not in the body of Christ).

How did Paul tell them to walk out their faith among outsiders?

These may seem like weird instructions to give for how to love those who are outside the body of Christ. Let's dig into this a little bit more.

+ **Lead a quiet life.** When the Thessalonians became Christ-followers, the work of Christ in their hearts altered their social, political, and religious circles. They couldn't do life the same way they had before. While they were to live differently than the culture around them, Paul warned against unnecessarily stirring up public controversy. They were to mind their own business and live with integrity. Paul knew that living a "quiet life" that earned the respect of those in society could ultimately open doors for the gospel.
+ **Work with your own hands.** Here, Paul encouraged the Thessalonians to be self-supporting, contributing members of the church and of society. He wanted them to avoid idleness that led to dependence. Their ability to support themselves as individuals would greatly affect the level of ministry they could contribute to as a church body.[21]

Paul's instructions were very specific ways that the Thessalonians could love those who didn't believe in Christ. The more they lived out a transformed life, the more people would take notice and ask questions. Ultimately, they were expressing love because they were living in such a way that others could see Christ in them.

What are some ways within our culture that we could express the love of Christ in how we live?

SHARE YOUR STORY

Challenge: *Valentines are exchanged as published displays of affection. What would happen if you gave a "valentine" out of season this week? Share an expression of love for friends and family.*

#FaithfulOne

Remember to begin with a time of prayer to focus your heart and invite God to truly make you alert to whatever He wants to teach you. As you read through chapter 4 again, be alert for how God is calling you specifically to honor Him in the various ways that are mentioned in the passage. Use page 55 to underline, circle, and draw as we work through the verses.

 Let's read specifically in verse 7-8. Circle the word *called*. In the margin, draw an old-fashioned phone. You know, the one with the dangling cord attaching the receiver to the dial.

How do you know when someone is calling you?

Think about the last few phone calls you received. What were they about? Who were they from?

There is something personal about getting a call from someone who knows you and wants to share information or news or just spend time with you. While they did not use phones in biblical times, the same concept can be applied when we see the word *calling*—when people were called to something in Scripture, it was personal and compelling.

I love the stories where Jesus called His disciples to come and follow Him. He often found them doing ordinary things like fishing, and He called them to leave it all behind. When He called them, He was inviting them to leave their old lives and find new lives with Him. In our passage for today, God called the Thessalonians to leave impurity and to walk in holiness. This was meant to be personal and compelling. It was an invitation to leave their old lives and find new lives in Him. Paul wanted to make sure the Thessalonians understood the importance of this calling.

Who did Paul say they were rejecting if they chose to ignore this instruction in verse 8?

Now circle the words *Holy Spirit* in verse 8. This seems like a weird thing to add at the end of this verse, but when you look at what God called the Thessalonians to, it makes sense. God had not called them to an impossible task. He knew that with the Holy Spirit, the Thessalonians could walk in holiness. The same is true for us.

Have you ever had a friend stand by you during a difficult event or struggle in your life? Explain.

How did having that friend there help you get through the difficult time?

I ran a half marathon a few years ago with two other people. My friend, Amy, was my coach. She stayed right by my side the ENTIRE race. She set the pace. She would encourage me and give me little goals to keep me running. "We have one mile left. That's 10 minutes. You can do anything for 10 minutes!" As I reflect on that race, it's a reminder to me of how the Holy Spirit works in our lives. The person of the Holy Spirit is alive and at work within us as we pursue holiness. When it gets hard—He encourages. When we need clarity—He sheds light on the path with Scripture. When we need strength for a task—He gives us His power to bring glory to God.

Here are three things I want you to remember about the Holy Spirit:
1. **He is infinitely intelligent.** (1 Cor. 2:10-11; Rom. 8:27)
2. **He has a will and purpose.** (1 Cor. 12:11)
3. **He works in a number of ways in our lives.** (John 14:16,26; Acts 1:8, Eph. 4:3; Gal. 5:16-25) He gives wisdom, peace, strength, guidance, comfort, and power. He is the One who empowers us spiritually in our pursuit of holiness.

What a gift God has given in providing us with the power through the Holy Spirit for the calling to holiness!

How does knowing you have the Holy Spirit walking with you impact your life's journey?

How have you sensed the Holy Spirit at work in your life as you've been reading His Word?

Are there areas of your life He has identified that are not bringing glory to God? Is so, what are they?

How will you fight the sin that is attacking your holiness and purity?

SHARE YOUR STORY

Challenge: *Post one of the verses about the Holy Spirit we looked at today. Let that be a reminder that He is always with us!*

#FaithfulOne

Today is the last day of reading chapter 4. Good for you! You've been at this for four weeks now and we are at the halfway point. I'm so proud of you and excited about all that God is teaching you! Keep it up, friend! As we dig in, we are going to tackle some pretty heavy (and much debated) theological verses. Are you up for the challenge? Remember to use page 55 to underline, circle, and draw things out as we go through this passage.

OK, let's lock in on verses 13-18. Underline the word <u>asleep</u> every time you see it. Write the initials _R.I.P._ in the margin. These were not extremely tired people Paul was talking about. We sometimes use the words _rest_ or _sleep_ when referring to people who have passed away because it seems less offensive to those who are grieving.[22] We also use those words because people who have died look as if they are sleeping. That's why you'll see the initials R.I.P. which means _rest in peace._

The Thessalonians had a lot of concerns about what happened when they died. They were also confused about their friends and family members who had already passed away. We don't often like to think about our lives ending because we have so much to live for in the here and now.

In the space provided, draw a gravestone. Write your name and birth date followed by a dash. Right now you are living in the "dash" period of your life. But our days are numbered. There will come a time when a closing date will be placed on that stone.

The Thessalonians believed that Jesus was coming back during their time on earth and they lived as if He would return before they died. As Christ-followers today, we don't talk often about Christ's return. And not many live as if He will return in our lifetime. We seem content to focus on living in the "dash"...the here and now. Think about the difference in perspective between the Thessalonians and Christians today. The time of Christ's return is nearer to us with each day we live. He could return today. We've lost the urgency that His impending return brings to the church.

Who benefits most if we as Christians lose the urgency to share the gospel and build up the kingdom of God?

Underline the word *clouds* in verse 17. Draw a cloud in the margin with a cross on top of it.
This particular word is what theologians call a *theophany*. It was not literal clouds that Paul was talking about. This was a symbol for the presence of God.[23] Even back in the Old Testament, in Exodus 13:21, the Israelites followed a cloud by day and a pillar of fire by night as they traveled. This was to signify that God was with them.

Paul comforted the Thessalonians with the assurance that those believers who had already died would not be forgotten. They would be resurrected to be with Christ. Our passing from this life to the next is a scary thing because we can't know for sure what it's like. But Paul gave words of comfort in the last part of verse 17. These words were for the Thessalonians as well as for us.

Who will be with us in the end?

Those who do not receive Christ as Savior during their lifetime will not be able to receive the comfort and peace of Christ at their death. There will be no presence of God for them. The absence of God's presence will be felt for eternity. These are sobering truths. And ones that should compel us to share the hope of Christ with the world while there's time!

How does the reality that people will die without Christ affect what you choose to do with your life "in the dash"?

We don't talk very often about our funerals or about the fact that our lives will eventually end. It's not something that we want to focus on, but there will be an end. Either Christ will return while we are living or we will breathe our last breath one day. Take a moment to think about your funeral. Will those who attend be comforted to know you are *always with the Lord* or will they grieve because you are unable to be present with Christ?

Next time you see clouds in the sky, let it be a reminder of God's presence and the comfort we have as believers as we wait expectantly for Christ's return.

SHARE YOUR STORY

Challenge: *Share about the source of your hope in life and in death.*

#FaithfulOne

SESSION 5

Children of Light

I THESSALONIANS 5:1-28

1 About the times and the seasons: Brothers, you do not need anything to be written to you. 2 For you yourselves know very well that the Day of the Lord will come just like a thief in the night. 3 When they say, "Peace and security," then sudden destruction comes on them, like labor pains come on a pregnant woman, and they will not escape. 4 But you, brothers, are not in the dark, for this day to overtake you like a thief. 5 For you are all sons of light and sons of the day. We do not belong to the night or the darkness. 6 So then, we must not sleep, like the rest, but we must stay awake and be serious. 7 For those who sleep, sleep at night, and those who get drunk are drunk at night. 8 But since we belong to the day, we must be serious and put the armor of faith and love on our chests, and put on a helmet of the hope of salvation. 9 For God did not appoint us to wrath, but to obtain salvation through our Lord Jesus Christ, 10 who died for us, so that whether we are awake or asleep, we will live together with Him. 11 Therefore encourage one another and build each other up as you are already doing. 12 Now we ask you, brothers, to give recognition to those who labor among you and lead you in the Lord and admonish you, 13 and to regard them very highly in love because of their work. Be at peace among yourselves. 14 And we exhort you, brothers: warn those who are irresponsible, comfort the discouraged, help the weak, be patient with everyone. 15 See to it that no one repays evil for evil to anyone, but always pursue what is good for one another and for all. 16 Rejoice always! 17 Pray constantly. 18 Give thanks in everything, for this is God's will for you in Christ Jesus. 19 Don't stifle the Spirit. 20 Don't despise prophecies, 21 but test all things. Hold on to what is good. 22 Stay away from every kind of evil. 23 Now may the God of peace Himself sanctify you completely. And may your spirit, soul, and body be kept sound and blameless for the coming of our Lord Jesus Christ. 24 He who calls you is faithful, who also will do it. 25 Brothers, pray for us also. 26 Greet all the brothers with a holy kiss. 27 I charge you by the Lord that this letter be read to all the brothers. 28 The grace of our Lord Jesus Christ be with you.

Intro

How often do you look up at the stars? When was the last time you remember observing the night sky? Take a moment and describe a starry night to the group or to the person sitting next to you.

What did everyone's description have in common?

Did anyone describe the dark?

It's the stars that stand out to us and become the most memorable. They shine bright and catch our attention. Even in the darkness, we can see these brilliant glimpses of light piercing through the black backdrop.

Today we are going to look at the picture of night and day that Paul gave the Thessalonians. He used familiar imagery as an analogy for the two ways of living in reality of the Day of the Lord.

Between the Lines

Use page 71 to underline, circle, and draw as we dig deeper into this passage.

In the last chapter, Paul shared some pretty groundbreaking information regarding the coming of the Lord. Timothy reported back to Paul questions the Thessalonians had about what Christ's return would mean for believers who had already died. They were concerned their friends would not be able to experience life with Christ in heaven.

As we'll see in chapter 5, Paul reinforced how the reality of Christ's return would affect their "now" as well as their "not yet." **Read chapter 5 together now.** Paul used three distinct situations as pictures to illustrate Christ's return. In the space below, write down how each picture could "shed light" on the details or manner of Christ's return.

   ✦ **A thief in the night (5:2)**

   ✦ **A military invasion (5:3a)**

   ✦ **A pregnant woman in labor (5:3b)**

In each of these situations, if you were not prepared, would you be able to delay the implications? Why or why not?

Paul began in verses 4 and 5 to associate his friends with daylight. All throughout Scripture, *light* is often associated with a relationship with Christ and darkness is associated with those who do not know Christ.

Underline this statement in verse 5: <u>We do not belong to the night or the darkness.</u>

Paul made the Thessalonians aware that there was another reality at work beyond the physical realm in which they lived. There were those around them that belonged to the night, spiritually speaking. They walked in darkness as ones who had not *received the Light*. Paul and the Thessalonian believers lived in opposition to the darkness; they belonged to the day because Christ had rescued them from darkness and brought them into His light.

Read Isaiah 9:2 and John 8:12 together.

What do these verses say about the source of light?

This idea of walking in darkness is one we can all grasp. Think of a moment when you were in the dark. What do you remember about that particular moment? How did the darkness frustrate, complicate, or cooperate with what you trying to do or where you were trying to go?

This is the picture Paul was communicating about the reality of living as light in a dark world. Because we are in Christ, we see clearly what it means to live in the now and not yet. Those who are not in Christ are unable to know their present circumstances are affected by their future reality.

Based on what we've read in chapter 5, who knows that the Day of the Lord is coming?

CROSS REFERENCE

The people walking in darkness have seen a great light; a light has dawned on those living in the land of darkness.
Isaiah 9:2

CROSS REFERENCE

Then Jesus spoke to them again: "I am the light of the world. Anyone who follows Me will never walk in the darkness but will have the light of life.
John 8:12

Perikephalaía:
Greek word
translated helmet.
It literally means
"head covering" in a
military sense[24]

THEME VERSE

*He who calls you is
faithful, who also
will do it.*
I Thessalonians 5:24

Who is able to make preparations—those who belong to the day, those who belong to the dark, or both?

Underline all the occurrences of the words *dark* and *night* in chapter 5 from verses 4-11. In the margin, draw a circle that is filled in to represent darkness. Next, circle the words *light* and *day* every time they appear in the same passage. In the margin, draw a star to represent light.

Once Paul explained the *day/night* realities, he gave clarity on what the people should be doing as they waited for the Lord's return. There is always a purpose in the waiting. And this kind of waiting looks very different than waiting on dinner to be served, waiting in the doctor's office, or waiting on a phone call. The waiting Paul described was an active waiting. In fact, he moved from this right into "battle" talk.

Read verse 8 again. Interestingly, alongside the battle talk, Paul highlighted three words we have over and over in his letter. **Underline faith, love and hope in this verse.**

Draw the two pieces of armor Paul figuratively wants the believers to put on.

What vital organs are being protected with these pieces of armor?

Perikephalaía is the Greek word translated *helmet*. It literally means "head covering" in a military sense. The idea is that the hope we have in salvation is so sure that it guards our mind like a helmet does for a soldier going into battle. We can confidently move into battle against Satan and the darkness around us, because our God is faithful and we know who wins in the end. Paul confidently reminded the Thessalonians in verse 24 that the Faithful One was the source of their hope. **Underline verse 24 and write *Faithful One* in the margin.**

Reflect and Respond

One of the cross references you may see in your Bible next to today's chapter is Philippians 2:15-16. Let's read this together and see how it reinforces what we've already learned.

...so that you may be blameless and pure, children of God who are faultless in a crooked and perverted generation, among whom you shine like stars in the world. Hold firmly to the message of life. Then I can boast in the day of Christ that I didn't run or labor for nothing.

How do you see evidence of the "battle" as you live out your faith in this crooked generation?

How does your relationship with Christ give you courage to live as a shining star?

For those of us doing this study, the mind and the heart are the primary battlefields that Satan will use to attack us.

How does God's Word protect our mind and our hearts in battle?

As a reminder that we belong to the light, draw a star on your hand as a challenge to shine bright in the darkness because you have a hope that will not fail; you have a Savior that has covered you with a sure future!

SHARE YOUR STORY

Challenge: *Memorize 1 Thessalonians 5:24. Post this verse as a reminder that HE IS FAITHFUL.*

#FaithfulOne

Before you get started, make sure you are in a place free from distractions and ready to dig into God's Word. Remember to turn off your devices or switch them to "do not disturb" so you can give Him all your attention. Continue using page 71 to underline, circle, and draw images as we interact with today's passage.

Begin this time with prayer to focus your heart on God. As you read chapter 5 for the first time by yourself, underline any words and phrases that leap off the page to you. Write a question mark or exclamation point in the margin of any verses that you want to explore a little bit further.

As we dig into this chapter, we get a sense that Paul's words are a continuation of what he had already been dealing with in chapter 4. Paul continued to elaborate on the Day of the Lord's return because the Thessalonians had so many questions. There were rumors being spread about how the end would unfold and these new believers were confused. Paul encouraged them not to worry about the day or time, but to continue preparing for the day Christ returns by living as Christ commanded.

Underline the phrase peace and security in verse 3. Write the words *Pax Romana* in the margin beside that verse. Paul was calling attention to a phrase that the Roman Empire had coined during the height of their rule. Rome was in authority over the Greeks. The coined phrase meant "peace and safety." This was a type of propaganda message that circulated among people to promote the idea of "The Peace of Rome." Paul was warning the Thessalonians not to put their trust in the government of Rome but in God.

Was Rome able to provide "peace and security" to its empire?

What does history prove in regard to putting complete trust in a government?

We are blessed to live in a free country. I have visited countries where the people are not free and know that the leaders of their nation do not have their best interests in mind. We can only imagine how frustrating and confusing that kind of life must be.

As great as America is, can our government promise us peace and security? Is there any evidence to show they cannot fully protect us?

As children, we used objects to comfort us when we were upset. What objects did you need when you went to sleep (blanket, pacifier, stuffed animal)? Go ahead and share—no one will judge!

As we grow up, we trade simple objects of security for more advanced things. What brings you a sense of peace and security right now (popularity, relationships, success)?

Do the things on your list bring lasting peace and security or a false sense of peace and security?

What label did Paul attach to the name of God in verse 23?

Philippians 4:7 says, *And the peace of God, which surpasses every thought, will guard your hearts and minds in Christ Jesus.*

His peace is a sure thing. This verse says His peace will guard our hearts and minds in Christ Jesus. Interestingly enough, our hearts and minds are the places where the enemy attacks most in an effort to cause anxious thoughts and emotional unrest. But the Lord is ready to defend us. The enemy's favorite spot to point his weapon is right where the peace of God covers. Next time you feel anxious, ask God to help you trust Him more deeply in that area. Give your worry to Him and let His peace and security cover you.

SHARE YOUR STORY

Challenge: *Share about an experience when your circumstances should have made you anxious, but because you turned it over to God, you had indescribable peace.*

#FaithfulOne

Pause and pray before you get started. Remember to use page 71 to interact with the text. **When you are ready, read chapter 5 all the way through again.**

It is difficult as a Christ-follower to wrap our minds around our future with Christ. The "not yet" remains a mystery in so many ways. The Thessalonians were trying to determine how to prepare in light of all the persecution they were facing. I imagine at times they would reflect on Paul's teaching or Timothy's encouragement and feel solid as a rock. Then, perhaps some rumor would come their way and their faith suddenly felt flimsy like Jell-o®. Paul wanted to give them some handles to grab a hold of so they could live with the hope of the "not yet" even on difficult days.

When you read this last part of 1 Thessalonians through that filter, you begin to understand some of these tricky verses with more insight. **Read verse 9 and circle the words** *salvation* **as well as** *Lord Jesus Christ.* **In the margin, draw the white flag with a cross to symbolize surrender.**

In order to obtain salvation through Jesus Christ, we must first wave the white flag of surrender. In some form, we are saying to Him, "I surrender my life. I need You as my Savior. I can't do this on my own." For those that have surrendered their lives to Christ, verse 9 confirms that we are no longer destined for wrath when we stand before God.

How often do you think about the end of the world as we know it?

What movies can you think of that have focused on the end of the world as a plot?

What would you do if you thought the end of the world was coming today?

The Thessalonians were living in fear of the future and seemed to be coming undone by that uncertainty. **Read verse 9 again.** Paul reminded them that their salvation was sure no matter what happened. He reiterated this good news in verse 10.

Circle the words *awake* **and** *asleep.* **In the margin next to** *asleep,* **draw our symbol for death (R.I.P.). In the margin next to** *awake* **draw a coffee cup.** So you won't be confused with the awake/asleep references here, Paul was clearly talking about those who had died and those who were still alive. For those who had trusted Christ for salvation, whether dead or alive, the reality of their future was the same—eternity with Christ!

You know what this means for Christ-followers today—regardless of whether we physically die or live to the day He returns...we get to live forever in His presence! That should give us hope in every circumstance we face here on earth.

Are you currently facing something that feels like "the end of the world"? How can the hope of salvation help you as you face that situation?

Salvation brings hope because the God who has saved us can be trusted to keep His promises. Look up the following passages. Next to each reference, write out what it says about the faithfulness of God.

+ **Psalm 89:1-2**
+ **Psalm 91:4**
+ **Psalm 100:5**
+ **Lamentations 3:22-24**
+ **1 Thessalonians 5:23-24**
+ **2 Thessalonians 3:3**

How does acknowledging the faithfulness of God help you through the hard times?

SHARE YOUR STORY

Challenge: *Pick a verse from the list above and post it on social media today as a reminder of His faithfulness.*

#FaithfulOne

Begin this time with prayer to focus your heart. Keep using page 71 to underline, circle, and draw as we go through the passage. **Go ahead and read through chapter 5 again.**

Today we will look at the section of Paul's letter that my pastor describes as that point when Paul started writing like he was running out of room and had more to say. If we were holding his letter in our hands, it seems as if there would be writing on the edges and around the margins with all his additional thoughts. This section does follow the ancient rhetoric where the author includes a benediction and final words.

It truly feels like Paul was passing on survival tips for the Thessalonians to hang on to in the midst of the battle while he was away from them. The first one that we'll look at today is fundamental to our lives as well as to the Thessalonians.

 Today we're going to focus on just one verse. **Read verse 17 and underline the phrase <u>pray constantly</u>. In the margin, draw the praying hands icon we used in chapter 3.**

What is your first thought when you read Paul's challenge to _pray constantly_?

Before you dismiss the idea and think there's no way to do this, let me encourage you to think differently about the way we pray. If you have a phone, pull it out and pick a friend you normally text every day. Take a look at one of your favorite conversations you had via text with that person this week. Now, figure up how long it took to have that conversation over the course of the day.

As we text, we bring people into what we are seeing and doing, even though they aren't physically there with us. We look forward to showing pictures and talking about our day with friends and family. What if you began to think about prayer like that? What if you began to think about prayer as little live tweets or an ongoing text conversation from your heart to God throughout the day?

There was a monk from the 16th century named Brother Lawrence. He wrote a book called *The Practice of the Presence of God*. It has wonderful insight. It is written through the filter of 16th century English so it is not an easy read. Brother Lawrence was thirsty for the presence of God. He wanted to know how to pray without ceasing. He struggled with how to pray and at the same time go about the tasks he had. So he began to learn how to invite God into everything that he did.[25]

If we are being honest, most of us struggle to live in a "pray constantly" mindset. If you are not already doing this, it will take practice. I encourage you to set an alarm on your phone that reminds you to pray. Or put a sticky note in key places you frequent throughout the day. Whenever you see those notes or hear your alarm, don't treat it like another thing on your to-do list. View these moments like a deep breath for your soul where you get to share with God from your heart about what you've been experiencing. As you begin to recognize that He is with you throughout the day, you'll start to hear from Him in your heart.

As I've learned to stay in constant communication with God, there have been times when I have sensed that He wanted me to go talk with someone about Him. There have been times when I have known I was supposed to change my direction and go another way. I haven't always understood what God was leading me to do or why, but I have learned to recognize His voice speaking to my heart.

Let's try that now. Here's your first practice...
Pray! Spend time talking to Him right now. Begin to practice the presence of God without ceasing; start looking for ways to bring Him into the conversation.

Let's walk through a possible scenario of how this might look for you.
Begin to pray for the people you see as you go throughout your day. Let's say you are walking into school and you see a group of girls that you used to hang out with...and they ignore you. You feel angry or jealous or hurt. Invite the Lord into that conversation. You're already having one in your mind about those girls. Say something like: "God look at my heart. Why am I feeling jealous? Protect my heart. Help me to forgive people who hurt me..."

And there's the really important part. The "..." Those dots mean there's more that needs to be said. There's more to talk about so the conversation continues. It's ongoing. I hope you enjoy developing this prayer habit. Praying you stay #faithful to it...see what I did there? ;)

SHARE YOUR STORY

Challenge: *Share about a sweet moment you have had with the Lord as you have spent time in His presence this week.*

#FaithfulOne

Begin with prayer. Remember what we talked about yesterday...keeping the conversation with the Lord going throughout your day. Talk to Him as you read through today's Scripture and notes. Let Him open your ears to hear His voice as He speaks to you through His Word. Use page 71 to record your thoughts and make notes as we go through the passage together.

Read chapter 5 again. Underline any words or phrases that stick out to you as you read.
Today we're going to look more closely at what Paul has to say about building.

I just got back from Greece and Italy where I had the opportunity to walk around some famous places of architectural history. There were ruins everywhere of buildings that had crumbled over time. There are teams of highly trained professionals that come in and meticulously try to repair and restore these ancient structures to just a fraction of their once-known beauty. The ruins are still beautiful, and it boggled my mind to think about the emperors and great thinkers that walked the same floors we were standing on. Some of these places were around when Paul was speaking to the Thessalonians. He would've seen the buildings when he was in Athens. Paul used the analogy of building as he talked about a different kind of building process in verse 11.

Underline build each other up and draw a brick in the margin to symbolize this building project.

Draw a brick wall in the space provided. Write the names of Christians you know on each brick.

Now, read 1 Peter 2:4-5.
Coming to Him, a living stone—rejected by men but chosen and valuable to God—you yourselves, as living stones, are being built into a spiritual house for a holy priesthood to offer spiritual sacrifices acceptable to God through Jesus Christ.

We are a part of a living building project. God is using our lives and the lives of other Christians to build His church on the foundation of Christ. The part I found really interesting is that we are called *living stones*. We don't just sit aimlessly in one spot. We are called to live and to do so in accordance with the building codes the Builder has put in place.

You can't just do whatever you want when you build a structure. It has to pass certain inspections. And if it doesn't meet those codes, you have to rebuild. Paul was telling the Thessalonians to encourage and build one another up in the faith so that together they could be stronger and more effective for the gospel.

When I was walking around Athens, I noticed several pieces of ruins in the path. I discovered that the official phrase for them was *stumbling blocks*. This makes sense for obvious reasons. There is also such a thing as a spiritual stumbling block. Scripture warns of the danger of causing others to stumble. Stumbling blocks have fallen out of their original position and now cause people to trip on their journey. As living stones, we have a responsibility to the other "stones" in the building. Our role is to encourage one another! Cheer each other on. Challenge one who is weary to stick with it so they don't fall or become a stumbling block.

Look back at the names you wrote on the bricks earlier. What are some intentional ways you can encourage and build them up in their faith walk?

Just like a building project has an intentional building plan, let's build out our intentional encouragement plan. Ask yourself these questions:
+ How do I see Jesus at work in this individual?
+ How has Jesus used this person to help me in my faith walk?
+ What needs does this person have that I could talk with Jesus about on their behalf?

Use the above questions to help you determine ways to build up that individual through a note, a gift, an act of service, or quality time. When we recognize that we are "united" and being "built together" through Christ, it affects not only our faithfulness to God, but also our faithfulness to one another as the body of Christ.

SHARE YOUR STORY

Challenge: *Encourage someone today. Let them know you prayed for them, share something you love about them, etc.*

#FaithfulOne

Today is the last day of reading chapter 5. This is the close of the first letter. I hope as you've listened in and read along to what Paul was teaching the Thessalonians that God has woven His message into your heart as well. I hope that as we've wrestled with some tough stuff, that you have grown deeper in your walk with Christ. We've got one more letter to dig into after this one, so stay with me! Use page 71 to make notes as we go through the passage.

Read chapter 5 and make note of anything that stands out to you as you read. By the sound of things in the final portion of this chapter, it appears Paul was trying to help these new believers build structure into the church and support one another in the roles they each filled. There was not just one leader over the church in Thessalonica, and yet it was not an "every man for himself" mentality either. They were healthy but still young in their faith, so Paul had instructions to help them grow as a body of believers.

Put a circle around verses 12-13. These verses contain directions for members of the church so they would know how to relate to those who were leading them.

What did Paul ask the members to do for the leaders in the church?
1.
2.
3.

Underline verses 14-22. These verses contain general directions for the whole church.

What duties did Paul highlight in verses 14-22?

 Let's end this week discussing rejoicing and thanksgiving. **Circle *rejoice* and *give thanks*. In the margin, draw the turkey symbol for thanksgiving.** I love Thanksgiving Day. I have memories of Thanksgivings from long ago, sitting around the table listening to my mom and uncles share stories. Often, they were stories I'd heard before, but I loved hearing them. It reminded me of how precious family is and how our families help shape who we become.

Paul knew that when Christ-followers develop the habit of giving thanks for the work of Christ, it becomes contagious. It brings encouragement and celebration even when there are difficult things going on around us.

Even as I wrote this Bible study, I had a team of friends praying for me. I would give them reports along the way. As I was writing, there were several major distractions going on throughout the process. We had pipes burst at our house, we had cars break down, we had sickness in our family, we had our heat go out three times, and the list goes on. All the while, this team was faithfully praying and pointing me back to what I had to be thankful for. It kept me focused UP on God instead of distracted by my circumstances.

Next to each Scripture reference, write what caused rejoicing.
  + **Exodus 18:9**
  + **Jeremiah 15:16**
  + **Luke 10:20**
  + **Luke 15:6–10**
  + **Acts 5:41**
  + **Philippians 2:28**
  + **1 Peter 4:13**

Notice that rejoicing isn't rooted in things like having a good hair day, a first kiss, a successful shopping trip, or even winning a game. These roots go down deep. These roots are found in the joy that only comes from Christ's work. That's why even in the midst of persecution or difficult circumstances, the Thessalonians could throw a praise-giving party to God. Their possessions, even their own lives could be taken, but nothing could steal their joy in the Lord and His work.

As you close out today, I encourage you to throw a "praise-giving" party. It's easy as girls to let our emotions control our day. When you focus on circumstances or temporary things, then you will stay on a roller coaster of emotions. However, when you see Christ at work in your circumstances and fix your eyes on Him, then you are able to rejoice and give thanks in the ups and the downs. Invite some friends over or take them out for coffee and lead each of them to share at least one story of how Christ has been at work in their lives. See what happens to the joy in that group!

SHARE YOUR STORY

Challenge: *Rejoice in the Lord. Share what God has done for you that you are thankful for.*

#FaithfulOne

SESSION 6

Faith that Flourishes

2 THESSALONIANS 1:1-12

1 Paul, Silvanus, and Timothy: To the church of the Thessalonians in God our Father and the Lord Jesus Christ. 2 Grace to you and peace from God our Father and the Lord Jesus Christ. 3 We must always thank God for you, brothers. This is right, since your faith is flourishing and the love each one of you has for one another is increasing. 4 Therefore, we ourselves boast about you among God's churches—about your endurance and faith in all the persecutions and afflictions you endure. 5 It is a clear evidence of God's righteous judgment that you will be counted worthy of God's kingdom, for which you also are suffering, 6 since it is righteous for God to repay with affliction those who afflict you 7 and to reward with rest you who are afflicted, along with us. This will take place at the revelation of the Lord Jesus from heaven with His powerful angels, 8 taking vengeance with flaming fire on those who don't know God and on those who don't obey the gospel of our Lord Jesus. 9 These will pay the penalty of eternal destruction from the Lord's presence and from His glorious strength 10 in that day when He comes to be glorified by His saints and to be admired by all those who have believed, because our testimony among you was believed. 11 And in view of this, we always pray for you that our God will consider you worthy of His calling, and will, by His power, fulfill every desire for goodness and the work of faith, 12 so that the name of our Lord Jesus will be glorified by you, and you by Him, according to the grace of our God and the Lord Jesus Christ.

There are so many social media apps coming out these days that it wouldn't surprise me if there was one solely dedicated to snapshots of flowers, plants, trees, or some vegetation. I know there are food apps, but what if there were plant apps? Imagine an app called "Plantstagram" where you can document all sorts of things about the plants you love. You can ask questions and get answers from others who have plants that are thriving when yours is not. And wait for it...when you like someone's post, you give it a "Green thumb" and if you don't like it you "Leaf It Alone." #boom #gardeningjokes

So today your group is going to be the tester of my new app, Plantstagram. Using the blank Instagram-like box below, do your best to replicate a plant, flower, or vegetation of some sort that you've personally planted, picked, or taken care of. In the status box, describe the outcome of that particular plant/flower/tree/vegetation and the circumstances that led to you being involved with its care.

👍 LIKE 💬 COMMENT

Looking back on your experience with that vegetation, would you give it a "green thumb" or "Leaf It Alone"?

As we begin the second letter to the Thessalonians, we are going to look at whether they've grown or if they are cultivating some issues that threaten their growth. As we "dig" in, begin to think about the Thessalonians growth like a horticulturist might approach a plant. At the end of our lesson, it will be neat to see what you observed in their lives, and in your own faith journey.

Between the Lines

Use page 87 to underline, circle, and draw as we dig deeper into this passage.

As we open up Paul's second letter to the Thessalonians, we see some similar themes to what Paul addressed with them in the first letter. It is apparent from the reports Timothy brought back that Paul had some specific areas he wanted to address with them. **Read chapter 1 together.**

From the very beginning of this letter, Paul was quick to point out how thankful he was for them. **Look back at verses 1-6. Circle *faith* and *love*. Draw the corresponding symbols that we have used in the margin.**

One of the signature traits that Paul used when he wrote was referencing things in groups of three. In 1 Thessalonians 1:3, Paul said: *...your work of <u>faith</u>, labor of <u>love</u>, and endurance of <u>hope</u> in our Lord Jesus Christ.*

You'll notice in this verse that before the word *faith*, he used the word *work* and before the word *love* he used *labor*. Finally, he used *endurance* in connection with *hope*. Paul wanted the Thessalonians to know that although they had received Christ, the process of faith, love, and hope was not done. There was more work to be done.

Now let's look back at 2 Thessalonians chapter 1. Circle the word *endurance* in verse 4. In the margin draw the symbol we used for hope. This word *endurance* is translated from the Greek as *patient endurance*. It is connected with the sure hope of what is to come. This is not a hope that is generated in our own strength.

Now circle the word *flourishing* in verse 3. The Greek word here is *hyperauxánei*.[28] It is a very rare word and the way it appears here is only used in this verse in the New Testament. It provides the Thessalonians with an agricultural picture of what faith looks like.

HISTORICAL CONTEXT

Most commentaries will date this letter at a fairly short time after the first. It would be safe to say that this second letter was received less than a year from the first letter.[26]

WORD STUDY

Hupomone: Greek word for endurance translated as *patient endurance*[27]

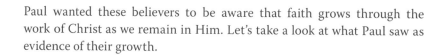

CROSS REFERENCE

In I Thessalonians 3:12, Paul prayed this: *And may the Lord cause you to increase and overflow with love for one another and for everyone, just as we also do for you.* Now we see the answer to Paul's prayer in 2 Thessalonians 1:3.

Paul wanted these believers to be aware that faith grows through the work of Christ as we remain in Him. Let's take a look at what Paul saw as evidence of their growth.

Love

Underline what Paul said in verse 3 about their love. This is a very interesting kind of love, especially in the culture of the Thessalonians. It seems like they were outdoing each other in the way they were loving one another.

Faith

Read verses 11-12. Underline what Paul said should be the end result of the work of faith. Paul's ultimate desire for this church was for their faith to bring glory to the name of Jesus. The same is true for us.

God is at work growing and transforming our hearts as we journey in this faith walk with Him. The depth of our love, faith, and hope shouldn't look like they did when we first responded to God's call to follow Him. When we grow in our walk with Christ, He gets the glory. We point people to Him because it's evident we couldn't cultivate godliness on our own.

That's what was happening in the lives of the Thessalonians. They were a "picture" of how God was growing and cultivating their faith. Paul could use them like we might use the "Plantstagram" app. He could say, "see how they were a year ago...well look at them now. That's God at work!"

How have you seen growth in your own life since starting this Bible study?

How have you seen growth in the lives of those you are doing this study with?

Reflect and Respond

We started out with our funny, fake app called Plantstagram where we could document how our plants are growing. What about the health and growth of our faith? How can we know when we are growing? Here are a few things to consider:

+ Is there an increasing hunger for God's Word and His presence?
+ Are you increasing in love for other believers and for outsiders?
+ Are you seeing evidence of the fruit of the Spirit in your life? (See Gal. 5.)
+ Another way to honestly evaluate your spiritual growth is to ask the people closest to you if they are seeing evidence of Christ at work in you.

We must be mindful of things that get cultivated in our hearts and minds that can choke out what Christ wants to do in us. I look at my heart like a garden and try to do a "crop check" on an ongoing basis.

What weeds am I allowing to take root in my heart? (Attitudes that are not glorifying to God, lusts, temptations, lies, deception, etc.)

What seeds do I need Christ to grow in my heart? (love for a certain person or people group, an attitude of humility, etc.)

Take a moment as we close out this session to spend some time allowing the One who knows your heart better than you to walk through it with you and point out how He is at work. Ask Him to call your attention to the weeds or seeds that need attention in your heart.

SHARE YOUR STORY

Challenge: *Share a picture of a flower or plant along with this simple prayer: Lord, help my faith to flourish.*

#FaithfulOne

Before you get started, make sure you are in a place free from distractions and ready to dig into God's Word. Remember to turn off your devices or switch them to "do not disturb" so you can give Him all your attention. Begin with prayer. Continue using page 87 to interact with the text.

Welcome to 2 Thessalonians! Let me help you get a little acclimated to this letter. It was also written by Paul and it echoes some of the same themes as the first letter. However, it goes into more detail and addresses some specific issues that the church of Thessalonica was struggling with.

As you read chapter 1 for the first time by yourself, remember to underline the words and phrases that leap off the page to you specifically. In addition, write a question mark or exclamation point off to the side of something that you want to explore a little bit further.

This week there will be a lot of "plant" talk. Which again is funny because every plant I have dies. I guess that makes me an expert in identifying what will kill your plants.
1. Not feeding the plant
2. Not watering the plant
3. Not placing it in the sunlight
4. Not tending to the plant's physical health (e.g., keeping pests away or treating for fungal issues)

So let's carry this analogy over into our spiritual lives. Paul pointed out in verse 3 that their faith was flourishing. Simultaneously their love was increasing. **In the margin, draw our symbol for**
❤ > **love increasing.**

So let's diagram this image. Draw a horizontal line in the space below. That will represent the ground. Underneath of the ground, draw some roots. Now draw a plant above ground, directly connected to the root system below ground. You can even draw little hearts like flowers coming off of the plant.

Here's the point: Just like the roots are the foundation of the plant, when the seed of salvation took root in our hearts, our faith developed and grew. The evidence of a root system below ground, is a plant above ground. The same is true in our spiritual lives—the evidence of the transformation within us can be seen as we bear spiritual fruit in our lives.

This theme of love increasing is a familiar theme. In fact, you should already have underlined the words faith and love with their corresponding symbols off to the side. Paul would not have said this exactly, but another way to understand this theme is by saying: Faith is the root, and love is the fruit.

Just like there are ways to keep a plant healthy and growing, the same is true for our faith. Here are spiritual disciplines that help our faith to mature:

+ **Spending time in God's Word feeds your soul.**
+ **Spending time worshiping God satisfies your soul.**
+ **Spending time in prayer shines light on areas of your heart that need attention.**
+ **Spending time with other believers provides accountability for your spiritual condition.** (My pastor always says, the first person we lie to is ourselves. That's why we need to be in community with other believers.)

Which of these spiritual disciplines are you growing in right now?

Which of these spiritual disciplines do you struggle to be consistent in?

As you monitor your growth, look at the condition of your fruit and it will tell you about the condition of your faith. Spend time today doing some fruit inspection. **Read Galatians 5:22-23 to see what fruit you should be growing:** *But the fruit of the Spirit is love, joy, peace, patience, kindness, goodness, faith, gentleness, self-control...* Remember these fruits are only grown by the power of the Holy Spirit in you. You cannot grow in your own strength. Pray for God to show you areas of your life where growth needs to happen.

SHARE YOUR STORY

Challenge: *Post Galatians 5:22-23 as a reminder of the fruit you want to see growing in your life.*

#FaithfulOne

Begin this time with prayer to focus your heart. Invite God to show you beautiful truths from His Word today. Continue using page 87 to underline, circle, and draw as we go through the text.

As you read through 2 Thessalonians chapter 1 again, you may end up with several questions. You will find a lot of vivid descriptions of destruction in this passage. As Paul handled questions about eternal life with Christ, he also had to deal with what would happen to those who never surrendered to Christ as Lord and Savior. One of my friends describes this reality like a justice scale. On one side you have eternal life. On the other side you have eternal ruin. The reality is everyone will face eternity and only those who belong to Christ will find acceptance in the presence of God. These are difficult truths we'll be wrestling with this week, but my hope is you'll be comforted as you more fully understand the power of His grace.

Read verse 5 and underline the phrase <u>God's righteous judgment</u>. In the margin, draw a symbol of a scale. The scale is actually a Roman symbol that was used to communicate truth and fairness in the Roman legal system. That is why the word *righteous* is so important in front of the word judgment. It's a reminder that the only one in a position to pass judgment is the One who is without blame.

There are multiple places in Scripture where God is described as a righteous judge. This is an important aspect to His character because it points not only to His righteousness but also to His authority as judge. One place in Scripture I want us to look at is Psalm 51. This was written by King David after he sinned against the Lord with Bathsheba. Read the following verse and take note of the powerful statement David makes about God.

Psalm 51:4 says, *Against You—You alone—I have sinned and done this evil in Your sight. So You are right when You pass sentence; You are blameless when You judge.*

God is a righteous judge who has the authority to punish sin and reward righteousness. **Now let's go back to 2 Thessalonians chapter 1. Read verse 5 and circle the phrase** *clear evidence.* Paul indicated that the evidence God would use to judge the Thessalonians was found in the fruit of their faith mentioned in the previous verses.

What evidence was there that the Thessalonians had been faithful?

What did Paul say they would be awarded with because of their faithfulness?

Read verses 6-9.

What did Paul say would be the punishment for the those who opposed God and did not obey the gospel?

There are definitely two realities presented in the chapter. A promise of eternal life in the presence of Christ, and a reality of eternal destruction away from Him. It's evident that when our "case" reaches the Righteous Judge, there will be no pleas. He knows the evidence of our faith and judges accordingly. Faith in Christ alone—in His death and resurrection—is the only evidence that pardons us. The Thessalonians had been transformed by that truth and their faith had endured in spite of persecution and affliction.

Can you remember a time when you said the words, "That's not fair!" What was the situation?

Fairness means everyone gets what they deserve. There is no favoritism. Sin has thrown off the fairness scale in our world. Christ's death and resurrection made a way for us to be pardoned in a fair court system before a righteous Judge. Payment has already been made for the debt of sin on behalf of those who confess with their mouths and believe in their hearts that Jesus is Lord. But there will come a time when those who never professed faith in Christ will stand before the Righteous Judge and receive His judgment without mercy.

Christ righted the scale for us. He took the sentence we deserved. If you have placed your faith in Christ alone for salvation, take some time to thank Him for His infinite grace. If you find yourself unsure of your salvation, you can pray to receive Christ into your life today! Trust the work He did on the cross as full payment for your sin. Trust in His resurrection power to give you new life. Submit your life to His lordship and commit to follow Him from this day forward. If you made that decision today, be sure and speak with a parent, friend, or church leader about this incredible step of faith! This is the most important moment in your life on earth. Let other believers come alongside you to celebrate and help you grow. You will need them just like the Thessalonians needed Paul and his companions to help encourage them in their faith journey!

SHARE YOUR STORY

Challenge: *Share one truth you learned today.*

#FaithfulOne

Begin with a time of prayer and ask God to keep your mind focused on His Word. Remember to use page 87 to underline, circle, and draw as we go through today's passage.

Yesterday we left off with the two realities of God's judgment. There is the reality of eternal life and the reality of eternal ruin. This particular passage does not spend much time on the implications of Christ's return upon the believer. **Read verse 10.** Here, Paul briefly reminded believers about the Day of the Lord. **Circle the words *glorified* and *admired*.** These are two words Paul used to describe Christ in that moment when His saints behold Him.

The believers in Thessalonica seemed to be unsure about what would happen to the rest of mankind at Jesus' return. **Underline verse 9. Pay close attention to the phrase *eternal destruction*. In the margin, draw a heart with circle around it and a slash through the circle to symbolize the reality that we are getting ready to explore.**

What are some of the images that you associate with hell? Draw them below.

Look at verse 9 again. As I have studied the reality of hell, it's not the eternal punishment that saddens me the most. It's the absence of God's presence—forever. Paul described this reality as *eternal destruction from the Lord's presence.* If the fruit of His Spirit is love, joy, peace, patience, kindness, goodness, faith, gentleness, and self-control...then in His absence, none of these will be found. There will be no love in hell. There will be no peace in hell.

We cannot grasp the horror of hell, but we have glimpses of what it will be like from Scripture. In Psalm 88:7-8, the psalmist describes hell on earth: *Your wrath lies heavily upon me; You have overwhelmed me with all Your waves. You have distanced my friends from me; You have made me repulsive to them. I am shut in and cannot go out.*

Because of the fall, every human can relate on some level to shame, loneliness, isolation and rejection. And there are days when we may wonder where God is when darkness surrounds us. These are glimpses of temporary torments here on earth. But hell is a real place where those who reject God will experience an eternity without His presence. It will not be temporary.

Pause and write down your thoughts as you process this reality. Feel free to write down questions you want to talk through in more detail with your parents, youth minister. or small group leader.

The reality of hell is overwhelming. But there is another reality at work. God's divine rescue plan has unfolded. Jesus conquered hell and now offers redemption to those who trust in Him alone for salvation. He is listening for the cry of those who call upon His name. His response is infinite grace and eternal life in His presence!

As we close, take a moment and reflect on the difficult truths we have wrestled with today. If you have already responded to Christ's rescue plan for your life, praise Him for His grace. Then spend time praying for those who have yet to respond to His mercy. Ask God to break your heart for the lost and to give you opportunities, even today, to share the hope of Jesus!

SHARE YOUR STORY

Challenge: *Share about the eternal hope you have in Jesus.*

#FaithfulOne

Begin with prayer. Use page 87 to record your thoughts as we study this passage. **Read through 2 Thessalonians chapter 1 again. Underline any words or phrases that jump off the page as you read.**

Let's start by thinking through a modern day illustration of something we will see in the lives of the Thessalonians. Think for a minute about "before and after" images. Our culture is fascinated with television shows about all kinds of transformations—we love before and after photos that document dramatic change. From home makeover shows to weight loss programs to fashion consultant shows, you can find just about any kind of transformation that interests you.

Have you ever watched a show like this? Which show?

What or who was being transformed? Was it a person, a house, etc.?

What about the show caught your attention?

Were the results dramatic? Explain.

Before and after stories inspire us to want that same experience for ourselves. Today as we look at 2 Thessalonians 1:10-12, we will see a before and after story hidden in the text. If you're not looking for it, you might miss it. **Underline the words glorified and saints.** The saints in this passage who are reflecting the glory of Christ were once sinners living as enemies of God. Salvation through Christ changes sinners to saints. Redemption is the greatest before and after story ever told.

Find 2 Corinthians 5:17-20 in your Bible and read it out loud.

The very first verse states that if Christ is in us, we are a new creation. The old things in our lives have passed away. We have a before and after picture. So what do we do with our transformation story? Let's move to verses 19-20. It says God has committed the message of reconciliation to us.

What is the message of reconciliation and what are we to do with it?

A good definition of reconciliation is to be *made right* with God or *restored* in our relationship with Him. So what does that look like for us to have this message of restoration put upon us as a new creation?

Read Colossians 1:21-29 to get more clarity on this subject of reconciliation.

Those of us who have been transformed by the work of Christ now offer our testimonies as before and after evidence of His saving power. We have been entrusted with the message of hope and now spend our lives helping others understand how Christ can make them new. And in the end? We get to be a part of the biggest before and after celebration of all time as we stand before the Lord reconciled—former sinners, now reflecting His glory alongside all His saints.

Record your before and after testimony. Describe your life before Christ transformed your heart in the BEFORE column. Then write about your life with Christ in the AFTER column.

Before	After

Satan will try to convince you that you are unworthy of reconciliation and restoration with God...but the Lord has a different message for you. I've personalized the following passage by removing the word "you" and putting a blank where you can write your name. Thank God for your before and after story!

1 Peter 5:10-11: *Now the God of all grace, who called _____ to His eternal glory in Christ Jesus, will personally restore, establish, strengthen, and support _____ after you have suffered a little. The dominion belongs to Him forever. Amen.*

SHARE YOUR STORY

Challenge: *Share how Christ has transformed your life!*

#FaithfulOne

Today is the last day of reading 2 Thessalonians chapter 1. Stay focused! Ask God to help you see all the things He wants to teach you through His Word. Use page 87 to record your thoughts as we work through the passage.

At different times during this study, we've come across verses about the persecution that the Thessalonians experienced. Most likely, none of us doing this study have experienced persecution for our faith like the Thessalonians did. **Read verse 4. Circle the words *persecutions* and *afflictions*. Don't forget to put a bandage symbol in the margin.** Paul was proud of how they were flourishing in the midst of the persecution they were under. In verse 5, he mentioned again that he was aware of their suffering. **In verse 6, underline the word repay and in the margin, draw tally marks.**

Now read verse 6 in The Message paraphrase:
When the Master Jesus appears out of heaven in a blaze of fire with his strong angels, he'll even up the score by settling accounts with those who gave you such a bad time. His coming will be the break we've been waiting for.

What are your thoughts after reading that verse?

My first year of college, our soccer team was pretty bad. I remember one game in particular when we played against one of the biggest schools in our division. These girls were impressive. The player I was supposed to track had a bad habit of trash talking to get inside my head. It worked! This team did not play fair. Our coach told us to watch ourselves because the girls would try to team up and literally take us out of the game by way of an "accidental" trip. They ran the score up so much that it looked like a basketball score. The game was embarrassing! I always wished we could have played them again after our team improved, but we never got the chance.

Have you ever felt like you were on the losing end of a situation? No matter what you did, you just couldn't seem to score or catch a break. Maybe it was a really bad day when nothing seemed to go right or a moment when you felt outmatched. Give a brief summary of the situation.

No doubt the Thessalonians felt like that at times as they faced affliction. In verse 6, Paul reminded them that even though the "scorecard of life" was being run up on them, God was in charge of payback. Verse 7 says that God would ultimately reward them with rest. God was not oblivious to the pain they had suffered. He not only took notice but He had a plan to deal with those who had afflicted them. God is our protector. He may not always stop the suffering at the moment we cry out to Him, but He is always watching over us and always working in the midst of our circumstances.

Remember earlier this week we talked about the fact that God is a righteous Judge. He will handle those who stand against us. And guess what? He doesn't need our help. Our job is not to do the repaying. Our job is not to take revenge.

Does that statement free you up or frustrate you? Explain.

Are there people who have wronged you that you still want to get even with? If so, create a mental list or write their initials below.

Guess what...you now have a prayer list.

Matthew 5:44 says, *But I tell you, love your enemies and pray for those who persecute you.*

That's what we are called to do with the scorecard. He'll handle justice. You just pray for them. And when you start praying for your enemies, you'll see God move in amazing ways. You might even become known for the way you love people—just like the Thessalonians!

SHARE YOUR STORY

Challenge: *Post Matthew 5:44 as a reminder that we are called to love, even when that is hard to do.*

#FaithfuLOne

SESSION 7

Faith Under Fire

2 THESSALONIANS 2:1-17

1 Now concerning the coming of our Lord Jesus Christ and our being gathered to Him: We ask you, brothers, 2 not to be easily upset in mind or troubled, either by a spirit or by a message or by a letter as if from us, alleging that the Day of the Lord has come. 3 Don't let anyone deceive you in any way. For that day will not come unless the apostasy comes first and the man of lawlessness is revealed, the son of destruction. 4 He opposes and exalts himself above every so-called god or object of worship, so that he sits in God's sanctuary, publicizing that he himself is God. 5 Don't you remember that when I was still with you I told you about this? 6 And you know what currently restrains him, so that he will be revealed in his time. 7 For the mystery of lawlessness is already at work, but the one now restraining will do so until he is out of the way, 8 and then the lawless one will be revealed. The Lord Jesus will destroy him with the breath of His mouth and will bring him to nothing with the brightness of His coming. 9 The coming of the lawless one is based on Satan's working, with all kinds of false miracles, signs, and wonders, 10 and with every unrighteous deception among those who are perishing. They perish because they did not accept the love of the truth in order to be saved. 11 For this reason God sends them a strong delusion so that they will believe what is false, 12 so that all will be condemned—those who did not believe the truth but enjoyed unrighteousness. 13 But we must always thank God for you, brothers loved by the Lord, because from the beginning God has chosen you for salvation through sanctification by the Spirit and through belief in the truth. 14 He called you to this through our gospel, so that you might obtain the glory of our Lord Jesus Christ. 15 Therefore, brothers, stand firm and hold to the traditions you were taught, either by our message or by our letter. 16 May our Lord Jesus Christ Himself and God our Father, who has loved us and given us eternal encouragement and good hope by grace, 17 encourage your hearts and strengthen you in every good work and word.

Just to get us thinking in the right direction for today's passage, I want you to pretend that you are an undercover CIA agent. Feel free to pick a cool spy name for yourself and create your undercover persona. You'll also need some of those fancy high-tech spy gadgets if you are going to sneak up on the enemy undetected.

What movies or television shows highlight the lives and work of undercover agents?

What qualities or talents do you possess that might be helpful as an agent?

What high-tech spy gadgets would you want to have if you were an agent? (Feel free to make these up.)

This picture of a highly trained agent will be helpful as we prepare to study 2 Thessalonians chapter 2. In this passage, Paul called attention to the false teachers and faulty information being used to deceive them. The church of Thessalonica was under attack and Paul wanted these young believers to recognize the battle they were in.

Between the Lines

Use page 103 to underline, circle, and draw as we dig deeper into this passage.

Paul began addressing the deception and lies that had slipped into the conversations among the Thessalonian believers. Their main concern, according to verses 2-3, was that the Day of the Lord had already come and they had missed it. Though Paul had addressed some of their concerns about the return of Christ in his first letter, they were still plagued with fear and uncertainty.

In our day, there are still a lot of questions and uncertainty about the return of Christ. We are not going to be able to answer all of those questions or delve into the different views about the second coming. For our purposes, we will stick to what Paul said in his letter to inform and encourage this group of believers. His words should continue to challenge and encourage us today.

Read chapter 2 together now.

Right at the beginning, we get a glimpse at how some of the confusion got started. **Underline verse 2.**

What were the sources of deception Paul highlighted?

The Thessalonian believers were confused and distracted. Whether by means of rumors, by unreliable messages, or by fake letters, the infiltration of false information was spreading rapidly. That's most likely why in chapter 3 verse 17, Paul was specific in saying this letter was written by his own hand. They needed to know for sure which message was reliable and true.

What happens when confusion and lies get planted in our minds?

HISTORICAL CONTEXT

Scholars are uncertain what is meant by the word *spirit* in verse 2. Some commentators believe this refers to a rumor that Paul had received a divine vision about the coming of Christ. Another source of confusion was verbal affirmation (a message) from the mouths of false teachers claiming they had spoken with Paul. Finally, the letter referred to was a fake, though some claimed it had been written by Paul.[29]

CROSS REFERENCE

This greeting is in my own hand—Paul. This is a sign in every letter; this is how I write.
2 Thessalonians 3:17

WORD STUDY

exapatáō: Greek word for *deceive*; common verb associated with Satan's traps[30]

WORD STUDY:

stēkō: Greek word for *stand firm*; combines the idea of standing in the Lord and holding to His Word[31]

Have you experienced a time when rumors or false information made things confusing or hurtful? What was the situation?

Once deception got into the minds of the Thessalonians, it started feeding conversations and creating alarm within the body. You've seen this happen before too. It may not be about the second coming of Christ, but your faith has been shaken or you've begun to believe certain things that are in contradiction to what God says.

What are some examples of how this plays out in our lives today?

In verse 3, circle the word *deceive*. The word *exapatáō* is the Greek word used here and it is a common verb associated with Satan's traps.

As Paul continued to deal with their questions related to the second coming, it became clear that the author of confusion, otherwise known as Satan, had successfully attacked with fear. Toward the close of this segment, Paul modeled what the Thessalonians needed to do in times of attack. He prayed for the Faithful One to bring peace and comfort to the shaken hearts of His followers. We can pray that same prayer today!

Underline verse 15. Paul used the Greek word *stēkō* for *stand firm* which combines the idea of standing in the Lord and holding to His Word. The picture he was painting for them was this: believers must stand on a foundation grounded in Christ instead of putting our footing in the sinking sand of this world.

Reflect and Respond

I don't know about you, but I have a plan of action in case there is a break-in, fire, or hostage situation at my home. I have never experienced any of these situations so it would be easy for me to say I'm not a target. Regardless, we had an alarm system added to our home that guarantees should any of these precarious scenarios arise, a skilled team of professionals will be sent to rescue my family any time the alarm goes off. The catch is, I have to turn the alarm system on to activate this protection. If I get lazy or forgetful, I forfeit the protection this alarm system offers.

We can apply this same reality to our spiritual lives in some ways. We have an enemy who is out to steal our joy and leave us cowering in fear. But we serve a faithful God, and daily we must turn to Him to be armed in this battle that we can't see with our eyes. He will provide the spiritual weapons and the strength to fight—we need only to lean into His authority and follow His lead.

Write out some areas of weakness that leave you most vulnerable to the enemy.

As we close today, use this prayer time with Him to help you practice turning on the "alarm system" of your heart. Everyday as a Christ-follower, imagine your life as if Satan has a target set on you. He is looking for ways to take you down in your weakest areas so that you are unable to boldly proclaim the message of Christ. As you spend time praying today, look at each area of weakness and reflect prayerfully on what temptations or struggles are at the root of those issues.

Father, we praise You for responding to our desperate need for You through the work of Jesus Christ. Thank you for listening to our prayers and helping us see You more clearly through Your Word. Remind us to be alert and to daily turn on our spiritual alarm system so we are ready at all times for battle. Thank you being an active, personal, and powerful God who cares about us. In the precious and holy name of Jesus, Amen.

SHARE YOUR STORY

Challenge: *Share some spiritual tools you will use this week to fight against confusion, deception, and discouragement.*

#FaithfulOne

Before you get started, make sure you are in a place free from distractions and ready to dig into God's Word. Remember to turn off your devices or switch them to "do not disturb" so you can give Him all your attention. Begin this time with prayer to focus your heart and invite God to truly make you alert to whatever He has for you to learn, confess, or live out today. Use page 103 to interact with the text as we study today's passage.

Read chapter 2 for the first time by yourself. Underline words and phrases that leap off the page to you specifically. In addition, write a question mark or exclamation point off to the side of any verses you want to explore a little further.

In verse 1, underline the phrase <u>coming of our Lord</u>. The Thessalonians got distracted by news and rumors concerning the second coming. They believed that the coming of the Lord would happen in their lifetime so they wanted to know how it would all unfold.

There are theories upon theories regarding the end times. Will Christ rapture or take those who are Christians and still living first before a time like the tribulation occurs? (Pre-tribulation). Or will Christ leave the Christians still living during His return to endure the tribulation? (Post-tribulation).

Pre-tribulation, post-tribulation, rapture...etc. These are really heavy conversations to have with believers. My concern: if we're having these conversations about the second coming of Christ with each other, are we also having conversations about the *first* coming with those who haven't heard yet?

Remember what the Thessalonians were known for in the first letter? If you need to refresh your memory, read 1 Thessalonians 1:8-9.

How do you get a group of believers who are on fire with the gospel to diminish in influence? **Read 2 Thessalonians 2:3.** We talked about the deceiver in our group session this week. Satan did not want them to be about the gospel, so he enticed them to focus instead on what would happen to them when Christ returned.

Last week's passage talked a lot about the reality of eternal ruin for those who don't know Christ. There wasn't as much of a focus on eternal life because the Thessalonians were already very aware of that reality.

How many people do you know personally who don't proclaim Christ as Savior and are not prepared for His return?

How often does their eternal destiny enter your mind or your prayers?

Why do you think we are not more urgent about sharing the gospel at all costs?

The Thessalonians didn't even realize they had gotten distracted from their primary purpose. They didn't see this attack coming. They probably thought because they were talking about things of Christ, they were doing the will of Christ. In reality, they were being delayed in their ultimate purpose.

What are some distractions that believers experience today that delay us from sharing the gospel with the lost?

The people you know personally who are not believers have been placed in your life for a purpose. The ultimate purpose for which the church itself exists is to make disciples by sharing the life-changing news of the gospel. Begin praying now for opportunities this week to talk with your friends and family about Christ. You may decide to call them, sit down face-to-face, or write a letter with Scripture references highlighted. Here's what some of our students did as a way of sparking spiritual conversations: they posted a picture message on Instagram letting people know they were available to talk with anyone who had questions about becoming a Christ-follower. They had a tremendous response! God used their obedience and there is evidence of changed lives as a result of that simple invitation to talk. Satan will try to delay you or get you to think you'll be rejected. Just remember, you have the boldness and strength of the Holy Spirit at work in and through you.

SHARE YOUR STORY

Challenge: *Consider posting an invitation for anyone who wants to talk more about a relationship with Christ to contact you. Remember, you may not have all the answers, but you have the Holy Spirit inside you and the Word of God beside you to guide the conversation.*

#FaithfulOne

Pray before you begin. Continue using page 103 to interact with the text as we go through today's passage.

? As you read through 2 Thessalonians chapter 2 again, it may spark some questions. Don't get too distracted by the mysterious man of lawlessness. **Read verse 7 and circle the word *mystery*. In the margin, draw a question mark to represent the mystery surrounding this name.**

What does verse 9 reveal about the man of lawlessness?

Now let's glance back at verse 2. Do you remember the tactics Satan used to confuse and distract the Thessalonians? Sending false messages was one of the attack strategies used to deceive these new believers. We aren't certain exactly what was said, but rumors began to spread among the church that they had missed the return of Christ.

What is the official definition of a rumor? I'll go ahead and tell you because I don't want you to find out from someone else. (See what I did there?)

> *ru·mor:* noun
> 1. a currently circulating story or report of uncertain or doubtful truth
> 2. gossip, hearsay, talk, tittle-tattle, speculation, word; stories, whispers, canards; informal grapevine, word on the street, buzz, dirt, scuttlebutt, loose lips[32]

Rumors are our specialty, aren't they girls? Even when we aren't the ones spreading rumors, we often find it hard to stop ourselves from even listening in!

Have you been a part of a rumor? Listening in counts.

Have you been the target of a rumor? Explain.

Rumors often seem harmless because we can't always see evidence of the damage they cause. For the sake of this illustration, let's think of them like matches that start wildfires. Once the fire is started, it is hard to trace the flames back to the original match. But the evidence of destruction is undeniable. What comes from our mouths can cause a wildfire of damage that can never be undone. Satan knows the power of our words. We can deceive, manipulate, and inflict pain with what we choose to say. And when this happens, we fall right in line with the enemy's strategy.

How did the rumors affect the believers in the church of Thessalonica?

After Paul dealt with the rumors circulating in the church, he modeled for them an alternative to rumors. He used his words to thank God for the Thessalonians. He used his words to encourage and build up the body of Christ. **Read verse 13 and circle the word *thank*. Draw the symbol associated with thanksgiving in the margin.**

Proverbs 26:20 says, *Without wood, fire goes out; without a gossip, conflict dies down.* Instead of rumors, spread words of thanksgiving and encouragement this week. Make an effort to talk to Jesus about the people who are in your life. Look for ways to point out how God is at work in the people around you and encourage them to keep flourishing in their faith. Before long, you will create a habit of building people up with your words.

SHARE YOUR STORY

Challenge: *Speak life into the people around you. Share words of encouragement that build others up this week.*

#FaithfuLOne

Begin by asking God to open your eyes to the truths He wants to show you today. Don't give in to the temptation to merely skim through the passage now that you've read it a few times. Stay in this and let His Word fill your mind and shape your character. Use page 103 to interact with the text as we dig deeper into the passage.

Read through 2 Thessalonians chapter 2 again. Underline or circle any words that stand out to you this time.

In the midst of swirling rumors and general confusion, Paul had to do something to stabilize these new, impressionable believers. He modeled for them a great strategy for attacking lies in the church.

1. He tracked down the sources of the lies (v. 2).

2. He identified what happened (v. 3).

3. He identified how it happened and reiterated their source of reliable truth (v. 5).

4. He highlighted how they could keep this from happening again (v. 15).

The imagery that comes to mind in verse 15 is one of trying to cross a raging river. If your group was out hiking and came across a river with raging waters, what tools would you need to cross over it safely? You may or may not know the answer to that, so I'll help you out. My husband is an outdoorsman and he shared with me that in this scenario, you would need a rope to get across safely. I did some research and found the safest way to do this. One person acts as a human anchor and holds the rope down from shore. Another person goes out into the water with the middle of the rope and a third person goes further down the shore acting as an additional human anchor. The rope makes the shape of a "V." As the person in the water moves toward the opposite bank, the human anchors give more rope until that person reaches the other side safely.

How important are the anchors in this scenario?

If the person in the middle of the river let's go of the rope, what would happen to her?

Now, read verse 15 again, but this time read it with the imagery of the rope in mind.

In the space below, write out doubts, distractions, and deceptions that could cause someone to be swept away from the truth of God.

In the midst of persecution and deception coming at the Thessalonians like a raging river, Paul told them to hold on to the traditions. **Circle *traditions* and draw an anchor in the margin.** ⚓ The word *traditions* in verse 15 is associated with trustworthy Christian teachings. We must heed Paul's words as well. We live in a world full of deception and distractions that threaten to sweep us down stream. The anchor that holds us is Jesus Christ. The truth that keeps our feet from slipping is God's Word.

After the last seven weeks in God's Word, do you see evidence of any of the following?
A. A deeper longing for the presence of God
B. A deeper love for the Word of God
C. A deeper knowledge of truth and understanding of what pleases God
D. Changes in your attitude and outlook on life
E. All of the above

The more time you spend in His presence and in His Word, the better equipped you will be to fight against the enemy's schemes. His Spirit will give you discernment to know the difference between truth and lies. And just like the Thessalonians, He will help you stand firm no matter what you face.

SHARE YOUR STORY

Challenge: *Share how God's Word has been an anchor for your life.*

#FaithfulOne

I'm so thankful we are on this journey together. There is still so much for us to discover. Begin today with prayer and thank God for His presence. Continue using page 103 to interact with the text as we go through the chapter. **Read through the chapter again now.**

Alright, all week we've been reading about the man of lawlessness and my guess is that some of you have already started doing your own research to see if you can figure out who he is. Maybe you've even developed a list of possible candidates. You can't suggest your little brother, your ex-boyfriend, or that teacher who gave you a bad grade. To keep us from getting too far off course, let's dig into what Paul shared with the Thessalonians regarding some of these tough prophecies.

According to verse 3, what two things must happen before the Day of the Lord comes:
1.
2.

Read verse 8. Put a box around *the lawless one will be revealed.* **In the margin, draw a mask to symbolize that his identity is hidden from us at this time.**

What can we tell about this masked man from verses 3-10?

We've determined before that this man of lawlessness (or you may hear him described in other places in Scripture as the "antichrist") is backed by Satan.

What can you learn about the antichrist from the following passages?
   ✦ **1 John 2:18**
   ✦ **1 John 2:22**
   ✦ **1 John 4:3**
   ✦ **2 John 1:7**

This commentary was helpful for me as I studied about this difficult subject. "Before the day of the Lord, a mere man will set himself up as a god. He will be backed by the power of the devil, fully unleashed because of the removal of the 'restrainer.' This means that while in Paul's day signs and wonders were proof of God's activity through the true gospel, in the end times they may come from the devil and be signs that lie."[33]

Allow me to illustrate that in a less academic way. Have you ever seen the old Bugs Bunny cartoons where Elmer Fudd is trying to get the hunting dogs to get Bugs Bunny? Bugs always does something clever to throw the dogs off his scent. It always makes the dogs look stupid when they fall for his tricks. There's an actual term for this in everyday conversation. It's called a "red herring."

> **red herring:** noun
> 1. Something that draws attention away from the central issue.[34]

So here is an interesting thought that I discovered as I was studying this particular passage. Often you find a community of Christians circle around a particular leader in the world to say..."that's him! the antichrist." Then nothing happens and years later there is another "antichrist" scare. Satan is a deceiver. He tossed "false messiahs" before Christ came onto the scene to get the Jewish people distracted. What if he has been presenting "false antichrists" through the years and in the present? The Thessalonians were pegging Roman emperors as "antichrists" even back then. Look what happened to them as a result—they were "shaken and alarmed."

What are the dangers of a *red herring* antichrist to the church of today?

Paul wanted the Thessalonians to stay focused on the certainty of Christ instead of being distracted by the mystery of the antichrist. Believers today are a lot like the Thessalonians—easily distracted and often frightened by the things we do not understand. Don't get thrown off course by the tricks of the deceiver.

What *red herrings* has Satan thrown in your path to get your focus off of Christ?

SHARE YOUR STORY

Challenge: *This world is full of evil, confusion, and deception. We can easily be overwhelmed by that if we take our eyes off the Faithful One. Post a prayer thanking God that we can be SURE of Him.*

#FaithfulOne

Begin this time with prayer. Today is your last day to read through 2 Thessalonians chapter 2. I know it's been a tough week with all this "man of lawlessness" and "deception" talk. But I don't want you to miss any of this incredible letter. Continue using page 103 to underline, circle, and draw as we interact with the text.

 Read through the chapter now. Slow down when you get to the end and take notice of how Paul wraps up this section. Circle verses 16-17. Draw our praying hands symbol in the margin. That's right...Paul wrote out a prayer for them—simple words etched on page. But more significantly, these were words that flowed from his heart.

Have you ever written out a prayer for someone you love? Explain.

Has anyone ever sent you a prayer (in a letter or even a text)?

How is writing out a prayer for someone different from just saying the words?

I can't help but think that the Thessalonians wanted to read this part of the letter over and over. They could probably hear Paul's voice as the words were read aloud. Just the thought of Paul praying these words faithfully on their behalf must have brought them a sense of peace. Paul intentionally placed this prayer after his big "man of lawlessness" section. He knew the church was shaken and troubled and he prayed to the only One who could calm their fears.

How did his prayer address their fears and questions?

Years ago, I went through a period of time where I had intense nightmares. I would wake up at two in the morning without fail and feel like something was wrong. I couldn't put my finger on it, but I was terrified. I knew that I was OK physically, but the fear wouldn't leave. I would call my mom or my friends and have them pray over me. When they did that...without fail...the terror left my mind and I was able to rest. In addition to prayer, I began to meditate on His Word. Verses like:

- ✦ **2 Corinthians 10:5 says:** *...take every thought captive to obey Christ.* (ESV)
- ✦ **Philippians 4:8 says:** *...whatever is true, whatever is honorable, whatever is just, whatever is pure, whatever is lovely, whatever is commendable, if there is any excellence, if there is anything worthy of praise, think about these things.* (ESV)

Thoughts that are not of God can float across our minds and catch us off guard. They can stir up fear and insecurity quickly. In those moments, we can pray God's Word and *take every thought captive*, then shift our minds to think about things mentioned in Philippians 4:8.

Even in his prayer, Paul instructed the Thessalonians to stand firm by thinking about good work and good words. He prayed a prayer of commissioning over his friends. He prayed that as they walked into difficult places and situations they would be comforted.

According to Paul's prayer, who would encourage and strengthen them?

And how long would that encouragement and hope last?

What a beautiful prayer. God knew that we would one day read these words and study these letters. He knew this very prayer would stir the hearts of Christ-followers thousands of years after it was first read.

So read it again, knowing that these words are for you too. Read it slowly and cherish every word.

I encourage you to pass along a written prayer to someone God brings to your heart. Use a part of this verse if it helps you know better what to write.

SHARE YOUR STORY

Challenge: *Post 2 Thessalonians 2:16-17 as a prayer of encouragement for someone God brings to your mind.*

#FaithfulOne

SESSION 8

He is Faithful

2 THESSALONIANS 3:1-18

1 Finally, brothers, pray for us that the Lord's message may spread rapidly and be honored, just as it was with you, 2 and that we may be delivered from wicked and evil men, for not all have faith. 3 But the Lord is faithful; He will strengthen and guard you from the evil one. 4 We have confidence in the Lord about you, that you are doing and will do what we command. 5 May the Lord direct your hearts to God's love and Christ's endurance. 6 Now we command you, brothers, in the name of our Lord Jesus Christ, to keep away from every brother who walks irresponsibly and not according to the tradition received from us. 7 For you yourselves know how you must imitate us: We were not irresponsible among you; 8 we did not eat anyone's food free of charge; instead, we labored and struggled, working night and day, so that we would not be a burden to any of you. 9 It is not that we don't have the right to support, but we did it to make ourselves an example to you so that you would imitate us. 10 In fact, when we were with you, this is what we commanded you: "If anyone isn't willing to work, he should not eat." 11 For we hear that there are some among you who walk irresponsibly, not working at all, but interfering with the work of others. 12 Now we command and exhort such people by the Lord Jesus Christ that quietly working, they may eat their own food. 13 Brothers, do not grow weary in doing good. 14 And if anyone does not obey our instruction in this letter, take note of that person; don't associate with him, so that he may be ashamed. 15 Yet don't treat him as an enemy, but warn him as a brother. 16 May the Lord of peace Himself give you peace always in every way. The Lord be with all of you. 17 This greeting is in my own hand—Paul. This is a sign in every letter; this is how I write. 18 The grace of our Lord Jesus Christ be with all of you.

Intro

How often do you come across a coin as you go about your day? How many coins do you think your group could come up with if you them all together? Now, even though the value, shape, and color of each coin is different, what is one thing that remains the same on every coin printed here in America?

Think about how many people carry the phrase *In God We Trust* around in purses, pockets, backpacks, even the crevices of couches and car seats, without even considering the implications of that statement.

For weeks now we've been looking at a particular group of believers who put their faith in God and trusted Him with their lives. As we wrap up this study, we must consider what it means for us to do the same.

Use the space below for a little coin art. Place a coin under your paper and rub across the indention with a crayon or pencil until the image of the coin appears.

As you finish your drawing, consider these questions.

When the world rubs against us, what indention will we leave behind?

Will it be a statement like the one on this coin—in God we trust?

Between the Lines

Use page 119 to underline, circle, and draw as we dig deeper into this passage.

Paul modeled prayer for the Thessalonians throughout these letters. In fact, he closed chapter 2 with a tender prayer asking God to encourage their hearts and give them strength. Paul gave them a picture of what it could look like to talk to Jesus about the things that were on their hearts. He taught them to pray for others and to pray with thanksgiving. He was constantly mentioning the Thessalonians to God and giving thanks for them. Now, he invites them in the first few verses of chapter 3, to pray on his behalf. **Read the chapter together now.**

What did Paul ask them to pray for in verses 1-2?

I.

2.

As he finished his prayer requests, Paul made a play on words. **Underline the statement he made at the end of verse 2 and the beginning of verse 3, For not all have faith. But the Lord is faithful.** Paul was aware that God's faithfulness did not depend on man's ability to obey. God is faithful no matter what. He is not going to let us down. He is a sure thing.

Our faith may waiver like a coin being flipped in the air, but God is never changing.

What did Paul say our faithful God would do for us in verse 3?

I.

2.

As often as Paul boasted about the Thessalonians, where did he put his confidence regarding his friends based on verse 4?

Verse 5 is my prayer for every girl and leader that goes through this study. The word *hearts* is the Greek word *kardía.* Most of the time, the word *heart* refers to our emotions, but here it means *the whole person.*

WORD STUDY

kardía: Greek word for *heart*; referring to the whole person[35]

What did Paul want the Lord to direct their "hearts" to?

1.

2.

After Paul encouraged them with these words, he made a shift in subject matter. Remember that this passage was originally part of a letter being written with Paul's own hand. He knew his letter was coming to a close so he continued to address questions and concerns.

In verses 6-15, Paul addressed issues of responsibility and reminded them of the example he and his companions lived out before them when they were in Thessalonica. He closed out the letter with a final prayer for peace.

Read verse 16.

Who gives peace?

When does this peace come?

How does this peace show up?

Read these answers out loud.
+ The Lord gives peace
+ Always
+ In every way

Peace is the product of trusting God. That doesn't mean our circumstances will always be peaceful. Think about the Thessalonians and all they had endured. They were persecuted and attacked from every side, yet Paul reminded them that peace could be theirs...at all times, in every way. Because the Lord of peace would always be with them.

The same is true for us.

Reflect and Respond

Paul prayed that the Lord would direct the Thessalonians—not just their emotions or their future steps—but their whole lives. He wanted them to lay themselves before the Lord, holding nothing back. This whole-hearted, all-in kind of life is not easy. In fact, it's impossible without the power of Christ working in us. Our response to His infinite love and immeasurable grace is sacrificial obedience.

So how do we know if we are following His lead? One way is to ask some questions before God to get a sense of where He is moving us and how willing we are to follow Him.

Have you sensed the Holy Spirit prompting you in any area as you've gone through this study? Maybe in an area where you have been holding on to control and need to give the reins back to God. Or an area of weakness where the enemy has a clear target to shoot arrows of shame or temptation. Or a goal or talent that has become an obsession and taken your focus off of God.

Write down whatever the Lord has been dealing with you about here:

Do you have an accountability partner who can pray with you and encourage you in the journey ahead? If so, thank God for that person. If not, would you consider finding someone you trust who could help you keep your eyes on the Lord?

As you move into your last week of study, commit to finishing strong. Don't miss a single truth God has for you. My prayer is that you will walk away not merely knowing more about the Lord but unable to imagine your day without His presence. My prayer is that you will continue to fall deeply in love with our Faithful One.

SHARE YOUR STORY

Challenge: *If you could share one thing with the world about the Faithful One, what would you say?*

#FaithfulOne

Welcome to our last week of studying 1 and 2 Thessalonians together! I'm so proud of the great endurance and faithfulness you've demonstrated in your pursuit of God's Word. Before you get started today, make sure you are in a place free from distractions and ready to dig in. Begin with prayer and don't forget to utilize page 119 as we interact with the passage.

Read chapter 3 all the way through right now. Underline the words and phrases that leap off the page. Put a question mark or exclamation point off to the side of any verses you want to explore a little bit further.

Throughout Paul's letters, he modeled for the Thessalonians the practice of prayer. He prayed consistently and passionately for them. Now in this final section, we see his authentic invitation for them to join in the conversation with God. This is an important aspect to his relationship with these believers—he didn't just pray for them, he opened a door to his own life and ministry in order to allow them to pray for him.

Do you have people in your life who call on you to pray for them? What is significant about being asked to pray for someone?

Underline the phrase that the Lord's message may spread rapidly in verse 1. Draw a tennis shoe in the margin.

As Paul addressed the Day of the Lord in previous parts of his letter, it's apparent here that he wanted the Thessalonians to feel a sense of urgency when it came to sharing the gospel. Since no one knows the day the Lord will return, we should feel that same urgency to proclaim salvation to the ends of the earth.

The imagery used here is a swiftness like in a race (which explains why I had you draw a tennis shoe). I love to run so when I start thinking of a mission attached to running, it makes me want to put myself in the shoes of the runner carrying the message.

Have you ever experienced a situation where you HAD to run? Explain.

How did you feel when you finally stopped running?

Did you make it in time?

I've had plenty of those experiences. Most of them had to do with catching connecting flights in large airports on different mission trips. One trip in particular, I was leading 20 students and leaders on a trip to England. We were going to miss our connecting flight to England if we didn't run. We ran hard and barely made it. When we sat down in our seats, people who had been waiting were completely unaware of the urgency that we had felt to get to where they were. They were oblivious.

Isaiah 52:7 says, *How beautiful on the mountains are the feet of the herald, who proclaims peace, who brings news of good things, who proclaims salvation, who says to Zion, 'Your God reigns!'*

Romans 10:15 says, *And how can they preach unless they are sent? As it is written: How beautiful are the feet of those who announce the gospel of good things!*

Both passages paint a picture of what it looks like for the message of Jesus to spread rapidly. These verses refer to the way a message was carried in that day and time. A messenger would run the news to the recipient. There was a sense of urgency and purpose in each step that messenger took.

As Christ-followers, we are the message bearers. We get the privilege of sharing with others what we know and love about the Faithful One. As I was writing this study, I had the opportunity to visit places like Greece and Rome. During those days, as I walked the roads that Paul walked, I prayed that the message of Jesus Christ would still be shared. Guess what?! God opened doors for me to share when I prayed that prayer.

You are a message bearer. I am praying specifically for you even as I write this. I'm praying you will recognize that you carry the message of hope and that you will be faithful to share it wherever He leads you.

Spend some time praying for different parts of the world today—start with our country, then expand out to other countries you may have visited or studied about. Pray for His Word to "race" across that part of the world and for the hearts in that region to be open to the good news. Pray that message bearers would stand up and race swiftly.

SHARE YOUR STORY

Challenge: *Continue to pray for different parts of the world throughout the day. Post the name of the country you are praying for.*

#FaithfulOne

Begin this time with prayer to focus your heart. Invite God to truly make you alert to whatever He wants to show you in His Word. Continue using page 119 to interact with the passage. **Read the chapter through again now.**

As we finish up the second letter to the Thessalonians, it's apparent that the majority of the believers were obeying the instructions and holding to the oral traditions that Paul had taught them. But there were some exceptions, so Paul addressed issues that were starting to surface among the believers.

In verse 6, underline the words <u>we command you</u>. Draw a conversation bubble in the margin that says, *Sir, yes Sir.* Some commentaries suggest that these words brought to mind a military imagery. Others just recognize that this phrase was used to get the attention of the listener.

In the military, what is the significance of a "rank"?

What is the role of the superior officer?

If a superior officer gives a command, what is the responsibility of those under his or her leadership?

Why do commands have to be followed in the military?

Paul was not inferring that he was superior to them by using this language. He did, however, want to catch their attention with the word *command*. He needed to communicate that following through with the instructions given was not an option, it was an absolute necessity.

Can you think of examples outside of the military where there are grave consequences if a "command" or "instruction" is not carried out with precision?

Read verse 6 again.

What were some of the characteristics of these "trouble makers?"

What was wrong with the way they walked?

According to verse 8, what did Paul point out about the eating habits they had modeled for the church?

Verse 12 echoes what we talked about in Week 4 day 3 about living quiet lives. Do you remember?

Read verse 14. Paul was trying to bring order to some disorderly people so he taught the church the means by which they should deal with those who did not obey. This was like a holy shun! While it may seem harsh at first, think about the consequences of not dealing with these issues.

How could "disorder" (disruptive attitudes, actions, and purpose) impact a church?

Paul used the body as an illustration for how the church is supposed to work together. The church in Thessalonica had some people who were not working in cooperation with the rest of the body. Paul taught them to deal with these issues with grace and compassion.

Think about your own church body. Draw the outline of a body in the space provided then label various ministries/leaders as hands, feet, arms, legs, eyes, etc. Think about the part you play as well. Pray that your church body would support one another and work together in a way that brings glory to God and expands the mission of the gospel.

SHARE YOUR STORY

Challenge: *Pray for your church leaders this week as they lead your local body of believers in a way that honors God and expands the mission of the gospel. Post a word of encouragement to them.*

#FaithfulOne

Pause and pray before you begin. Keep underlining, circling, and drawing on page 119 as we dig deeper into the passage today. **Read the chapter all the way through now.**

(Ⓩ) **Let's focus on verse 6 again. Underline** keep away from every brother who walks irresponsibly. **In the margin, draw the letter Z and put a circle around it.** Okay, this is going to sound crazy at first, but I want you to use that Z symbol to represent a zombie.

I'm not talking Zechariah 14:12 kind of zombieness where it says, *This will be the plague the Lord strikes all people with who warred against Jerusalem: their flesh will rot while they stand on their feet, their eyes will rot in their sockets, and their tongues will rot in their mouths.*

But as I read the words from Paul in chapter three, I can't shake the image of a zombie. These disruptive disciples had some characteristics comparable to a zombie. They were walking without purpose. It appears they were just wasting the day away. They were irresponsible in how they used the time they had been given. These idle disciples were most likely putting their lives on hold waiting for Christ to return. As a result, they were taking advantage of the rest of the body—eating people's bread without paying for it.

Why do you think they did this?

Verse 10 gives us a clue—they have no money to spend on bread because they had not worked to earn any wages. These disciples were just consumers. Now here's the connection to zombies. They walked around looking for life to consume. They did not add to anyone else's life. They were content to take from others with no regard for how that would impact the unity and mission of the church.

What are some ways we might appear like zombies every Sunday at church?

Are you the kind of person who consumes without giving back to the life and ministry of the church?

One of my favorite verses in this chapter is toward the end. **Read verse 13. Underline the whole verse and let the words sink in.**

For those in the church who were serving diligently, having consumer Christians wreaking havoc on the ministry meant they had to work even harder to make up the difference. It would not have taken long for the faithful Thessalonian believers to begin to feel weary. And weariness can tempt us to quit. This is why Paul's words were so timely and personal.

Have you ever found yourself "weary" from serving in different leadership roles within your church? Or maybe you serve behind the scenes where no one notices.

How are you currently serving the body of Christ and blessing other believers?

A favorite illustration of mine is the Dead Sea. The Dead Sea is incapable of fostering any life because of the high content of saltwater that is flowing into it. It is constantly receiving and it has no outlets where it can overflow into other bodies of water. It only takes, it never gives back. This is the picture we get from Paul's description of these irresponsible believers.

I'm praying for you as you consider the areas of your life that mimic the consumer zombie or the Dead Sea. Ask God to help you see areas that need to develop outlets of service. If you are currently serving and feeling weary, remember that He is faithful and He will give you the strength and energy you need to do the work He has called you to.

SHARE YOUR STORY

Challenge: *Memorize 2 Thessalonians 3:13. Post this verse as a reminder that He is faithful to provide for us as we serve the body of Christ.*

#FaithfulOne

Pray for God to focus your heart on Him as you read His Word today. Use page 119 to capture your thoughts, questions, and notes as we dig into the study. **Read through the chapter now.**

There are so many rich verses, one right after another, in this last chapter. As I was praying through which ones to dig deeper into, verse 14 came to my attention. **Read verse 14 and underline the phrase <u>don't associate with him</u>. In the margin, write the word *shun*.** Some of you may know what shun means, but let's look at an official definition:

> *shun (shŭn):* verb
> shunned, shun·ning, shuns
> 1. To avoid deliberately; keep away from.[36]

Paul ordered a holy shunning for those who continued to disobey. This was an example of church discipline. Remember that this letter was being read out loud to the whole church. Imagine if you were there and sitting next to one of the "troublemakers." #awkward

When I was in preschool, there was a rug called "The Pink Rug." Now, the pink rug might sound fun, but it was actually where you would go if you broke the preschool rules. One particular day, a kid in my class was picking on me. I was minding my own business when he yelled a comment at me about my hair being short. He said: "boys don't wear ribbons." Whoa. Fella. THOSE are fighting words. I reacted by throwing something at him. I had never sat on the Pink Rug before, and I never did after that incident...but on that particular day I found myself surrounded by pink. The real punishment wasn't the rug itself, it was the fact that you weren't allowed to talk to anyone and no one was allowed to talk to you. You just had to watch everyone playing and going on without you. This was my first experience with the concept of being shunned.

Paul incorporated a holy pink rug rule for those who did not hold true to what they had been taught. It reinforced the order that the church needed in order to function. It wasn't a rule created to hurt people, it was actually all about pulling people back when they had veered off course.

How could this apply to your group or your church today?

Sometimes we need a timeout in girls ministry! Bullying and the "mean girl" mentality can get out of hand very quickly. All too often, we let our emotions get the best of us and act out in ways that cause disunity. Not only does it cause a distraction from our real purpose as believers, but it can also leave painful scars on those who are suffer the brunt of that disruptive behavior.

How could verses 14-15 help us regain some holy order in a disorderly situation?

As we close out today, think about what it means to place boundaries in relationships that are unhealthy for you spiritually. The Pink Rug was an early way of creating boundaries. I learned we don't throw things at boys who are mean. But as I've grown up, I have had to learn to set new boundaries and bring healthy order to my friendships and relationships.

The girls in your church are sisters in Christ. You are commanded to love them. But just as Paul taught the Thessalonians, you must also be careful not to let someone else's disruptive behavior pull you off course. Healthy boundaries should not serve as barriers, but rather as bumpers that help us spur one another on.

What boundaries do you need to put in place to ensure healthy relationships with your sisters in Christ?

SHARE YOUR STORY

Challenge: *Say "thank you" publicly to mentors and accountability partners who have loved you enough to correct you in moments when you veered off course spiritually.*

#FaithfulOne

Well we've arrived, friend! It's the last day. You deserve a high-five for being so faithful to this commitment. I hope that you have enjoyed listening in on these letters from Paul to his friends in Thessalonica. As we conclude today, take some time to flip back through your book and reflect on all the highlighted verses, notes, and images that represent what you've learned.

Was there a particular theme that kept coming back to you as you hung out in 1 and 2 Thessalonians?

While the lessons are still fresh on your mind, make notes regarding commitments, prayers, or responses you made during this study. Share those with someone or let others who are doing the study know what you learned by using our study hashtag: #FaithfulOne. You might also enjoy looking at what others have posted on social media using that hashtag.

Alright, let's do this one more time! Before you get started, make sure you are in a place free from distractions and ready to dig into God's Word. Begin with prayer to focus your heart. Use page 119 to interact with the text as we wrap up our study. **Read through the chapter now.**

Paul closed out his letter with another prayer. **Read verse 16 again. Underline the phrase the Lord.**

We talked in the group session about this prayer, but let's dig a little deeper today. Not only did Paul pray for the Thessalonians to experience God's peace, he prayed for a peace without boundaries. Think about that for a moment.
+ A peace that cannot be stopped
+ A peace that will not run out
+ A peace that does not grow weary

Why do you think he prayed for that kind of peace to fall on the Thessalonians?

The word *peace* was a very important word to the Jews. It signified a wholeness that only God could bring. To understand this peace better, let's look at one of my favorite stories.

Read Mark 5:24-34.

In this passage, we are introduced to a woman who suffered from a medical condition that caused her to bleed for 12 years in a row. She had gone through all of her money trying to be healed by doctors. She heard about Jesus and the miracles He had done. In a crowded area where plenty of people were bumping up against Jesus, this woman believed that if she could just touch His robe, then she would be healed. Jesus felt her touch of faith. And He responded like this: *Daughter, He said to her, your faith has made you well. Go in peace and be free from your affliction.*

The Greek word for *peace* is *eirenē*. It means "when all essential parts are joined together." This is God's wholeness. And the word for *well* means salvation.[37] This woman's faith led to her salvation which brought her soul into one piece...complete. Wholeness through Christ. This peace is not an attitude or temporary relief from chaos. It is a state of being. It is a wholeness that holds our lives together no matter the circumstances.

Paul used the same Greek word for peace, *eirenē*, in 2 Thessalonians 3:16.

What about you? Have you experienced the peace of God that makes you whole?

This peace that passes understanding is yours if you belong to Jesus. **Circle the words *Lord of peace* in verse 16 and write WHOLE in the margin to remind you that He heals our brokenness.**

Are there pieces of "brokenness" you need Him to mend?

Are there fears, lies, and deceptions that you need His peace to cover over?

As His daughter, you can live complete. Just surrender your pieces to Him. *He who calls you is faithful!* End by thanking the Lord for His faithfulness—be specific as you recount the ways He has shown His goodness and glory to you.

SHARE YOUR STORY

Challenge: *Share how the Lord has been faithful to you over the past eight weeks.*

#FaithfulOne

Sources

1. Stanley E. Porter, *HCSB Study Bible Study Notes* (Nashville, TN: Holman Bible Publishers, 2010), 1895.

2. James Strong, *New Strong's Concise Dictionary of the Words in the Greek Testament,* (Nashville, TN: Thomas Nelson Publishers, 1995), 58.

3. E.D. Radmacher, R.B. Allen, and H.W. House, *The Nelson Study Bible: New King James Version*, 1 Thess. 1:6. (Nashville, TN: Thomas Nelson, 2012).

4. Robertson, A.T. *Word Pictures in the New Testament,* 1 Thess. 1:7. (Nashville, TN: Holman Reference, 2000).

5. H. Liddell, *A Lexicon: Abridged from Liddell and Scott's Greek-English Lexicon* (Oak Harbor, WA: Logos Research Systems, Inc., 1996), 824.

6. Strong, *New Strong's Concise Dictionary of the Words in the Greek Testament,* 46.

7. J.P. Louw and E.A. Nida, *Greek-English Lexicon of the New Testament: Based on Semantic Domains*, Vol. 2. (New York: United Bible Societies, 1996), 101.

8. Strong, *New Strong's Concise Dictionary of the Words in the Greek Testament,* 49.

9. G. Kittel, G. Freidrich, and G.W. Bromiley, *Theological Dictionary of the New Testament* (Grand Rapids, MI: W.B. Erdmans, 1985).

10. J.D. Barry, et. al., *Faithlife Study Bible,* 1 Thess. 2:9. (Bellingham, WA: Logos Bible Software, 2012).

11. Lahle Wolfe, *Biography of Leslie Scott, Inventor of Jenga and Co-Founder of Oxford Games,* [cited 14 March 2014]. Available from the Internet: *http://womeninbusiness.about.com.*

12. Strong, *New Strong's Concise Dictionary of the Words in the Greek Testament,* 80.

13. Ibid., 83.

14. John F. Walvoord and Roy B. Zuck, *The Bible Knowledge Commentary: An Exposition of the Scriptures,* 1 Thess. 3:10. (Wheaton, IL: Victor Books, 1985).

15. David S. Dockery, ed., *Holman Bible Handbook,* (Nashville, TN: Holman Bible Publishers, 1992), 729.

16. WayMakers, *Prayer Walking,* [cited 14 March 2014]. Available from the Internet: *waymakers.org.*

17. Gary Shogren, *Exegetical Commentary on the New Testament, 1 and 2 Thessalonians,* ed. Clinton E. Arnold, (Nashville, TN: Zondervan, 2012).

18. Strong, *New Strong's Concise Dictionary of the Words in the Greek Testament,* 70.

19. Ada Lum, *Luke: New Hope, New Joy* (Westmont, IL: InterVarsity Press, 2001), 27.

20. E.D. Radmacher, *The Nelson Study Bible: New King James Version,* 1 Thess. 4:5.

21. D. Michael Martin, *The New American Commentary, 1, 2 Thessalonians,* (Nashville, TN: Broadman & Holman Publishers, 1995), 135-140.

22. Barry, *Faithlife Study Bible.*

23. Ibid.

24. Kittel, *Theological Dictionary of the New Testament,* 74.

25. Robert M. Johnston, *The Devotional Life of Brother Lawrence,* Ministry Magazine, [cited 14 March 2014]. Available from the Internet: *ministrymagazine.org.*

26. Walvoord, *The Bible Knowledge Commentary: An Exposition of the Scriptures,* 712-713.

27. Strong, *New Strong's Concise Dictionary of the Words in the Greek Testament,* 94.

28. Strong, *New Strong's Concise Dictionary of the Words in the Greek Testament,* 93.

29. W. MacDonald, *Believer's Bible Commentary: Old and New Testaments,* ed. A. Farstad, (Nashville, TN: Thomas Nelson, 1995), 2053.

30. Strong, *New Strong's Concise Dictionary of the Words in the Greek Testament,* 32.

31. Strong, *New Strong's Concise Dictionary of the Words in the Greek Testament,* 83.

32. "Rumor," *Oxford Dictionaries,* [cited 14 March 2014]. Available from the Internet: *http://www.oxforddictionaries.com.*

33. Gary Shogren, *Exegetical Commentary on the New Testament, 1 and 2 Thessalonians,* 295.

34. "Red herring," *The Free Dictionary,* [cited 14 March 2014]. Available from the Internet: *http://www.thefreedictionary.com.*

35. Strong, *New Strong's Concise Dictionary of the Words in the Greek Testament,* 45

36. "Shun," *The Free Dictionary,* [cited 14 March 2014]. Available from the Internet: *http://www.thefreedictionary.com.*

37. Strong, *New Strong's Concise Dictionary of the Words in the Greek Testament,* 27.

Leader Guide

✤ Welcome (5 minutes)

Greet girls as they arrive and ask them to share highlights from their week.

✤ Video (10 minutes)

Watch the Session One video (included in the DVD Kit). Allow for discussion afterward.

✤ Opening Illustration/Activity (10 minutes)

It's hard to imagine a world without instant communication, but just for fun, let's pretend those methods don't exist right now. Instruct your girls to write a note to someone else in the group using old fashioned forms of communication. Provide index cards and pens; to ensure every girl gets a note, write the name of each girl on the cards. Pass the cards out at random. Tell them to write a short message (about any subject matter) to the girl listed on their card. Before they start writing, share with them that they will have three options for how they want to send that message:

- **Message in a bottle:** Girls who choose this option will place the message in a bottle—have a few empty water bottles on hand for this purpose. Once they seal their note, collect the bottles. Instruct girls to close their eyes while you hide the bottles around the room. This will represent how vast the ocean is and how difficult it would be for someone to find a message floating in a bottle. Give girls 1 minute to find and deliver bottles to the correct recipients.
- **Airmail:** Girls who choose this option will make a paper airplane using the index card. They must attempt to fly the paper airplane to the intended recipient across the room.
- **Message by courier:** Girls who choose this option will whisper their message to you as the "courier." You will travel by foot to the intended recipient and proclaim the message from memory.

Transitional statement: Today we begin reading the first of two letters written by the apostle Paul to a group of new believers in Thessalonica. These were hand-written messages with words that carried eternal significance. We don't want to pick these up and read them like a message in a bottle that we merely stumbled upon—we want to dig deep into the context (who, what, why) and enjoy the beautiful imagery and rich truths waiting to be discovered. Let's begin our journey.

✤ Between the Lines (20 minutes)

Read through the historical context and word studies used throughout the session (pp. 9-10). Highlight the information you want to cover with the girls as you study and prepare. Use the questions in this section to spark discussion. Encourage girls to use the Scripture page (p. 7) to underline, circle, and draw in the margin as you go through the passage.

✤ Reflect and Respond (10 minutes)

Consider splitting girls into smaller groups or pairs to discuss the application questions and challenges in this section (p. 11). After a few minutes of discussion, end with prayer.

✤ Closing

Before the girls leave, encourage them to complete the Share Your Story challenge (p. 11). Also encourage them to dig into the five days of Going Deeper devotions included in the book (pp. 12-21).

✦ Welcome (5 minutes)

Greet girls as they arrive and ask them to share highlights from their week. Allow them to share any thoughts or questions from this past week's Going Deeper devotions.

✦ Video (10 minutes)

Watch the Session Two video (included in the DVD Kit). Allow for discussion afterward.

✦ Opening Illustration/Activity (10 minutes)

Bring several items that visually illustrate something full vs. something empty. For example, you could place empty candy wrappers next to identical unwrapped candies; or empty glasses next to glasses that are filled with water; or an empty purse next to one filled with objects. Ask girls to describe the differences between the items and the implications of those differences. Inquire if any of the girls have ever seen a piñata. If so, ask someone to describe the object and the game that goes along with it. If you can physically bring a piñata to the meeting, allow girls to take turns swinging at it with blindfolds on. Let them enjoy the candy inside once it has been broken open. Use the questions on pages 24-25 to guide discussion of the illustration.

Transitional statement: In some ways we are like that piñata—we are on display for the world to see. When life hits us hard, our faith will serve as evidence of our relationship with Jesus Christ. We must be careful not to merely claim Christ as our hope when life is good, then fall to pieces when difficult circumstances hit. People want to know our hope is real and that the message we proclaim is filled with genuine faith in the One we claim as Lord and Savior.

✦ Between the Lines (20 minutes)

Read through the historical context and word studies used throughout the session (pp. 25-27). Highlight the information you want to cover with the girls as you study and prepare. Use the questions in this section to spark discussion. Encourage girls to use the Scripture page (p. 23) to underline, circle, and draw in the margin as you go through the passage.

✦ Reflect and Respond (10 minutes)

Consider splitting girls into smaller groups or pairs to discuss the application questions and challenges in this section (p. 27). After a few minutes of discussion, end with prayer.

✦ Closing

Before the girls leave, encourage them to complete the Share Your Story challenge (p. 27). Also encourage them to dig into the five days of Going Deeper devotions included in the book (pp. 28-37).

✦ Welcome (5 minutes)

Greet girls as they arrive and ask them to share highlights from their week. Allow them to share any thoughts or questions from this past week's Going Deeper devotions.

✦ Video (10 minutes)

Watch the Session Three video (included in the DVD Kit). Allow for discussion afterward.

✦ Opening Illustration/Activity (10 minutes)

If possible, bring the board game Jenga® to the group meeting. Hand each girl several blocks and a marker (cover the blocks with strips of masking tape that can be taken off after the illustration). Instruct girls to write ideas on the blocks for how someone might encourage them in their faith walk. For example: words of encouragement, leadership opportunities, prayer support, accountability. Play a game of Jenga using those blocks. In the game, you will start with a sturdy tower, then players will take blocks from the tower and add them to the top. The tower will eventually get shaky and unstable when pivotal support blocks are removed. This tangible illustration should enhance the learning experience as you challenge them to make spiritual applications from this activity.

Transitional statement: We all need a sturdy foundation (Christ) and other believers to come alongside to help us "build" our faith. The apostle Paul knew that the persecution the Thessalonians were undergoing would cause even the strongest Christ-follower to be shaken. He knew they needed support and encouragement to help build them up. Paul sent Timothy to remind them of their foundation in Christ and to help develop their faith so they could endure when persecution came against them.

✦ Between the Lines (20 minutes)

Read through the historical context and word studies used throughout the session (pp. 41-42). Highlight the information you want to cover with the girls as you study and prepare. Use the questions in this section to spark discussion. Encourage girls to use the Scripture page (p. 39) to underline, circle, and draw in the margin as you go through the passage.

✦ Reflect and Respond (10 minutes)

Consider splitting girls into smaller groups or pairs to discuss the application questions and challenges in this section (pp. 42-43). After a few minutes of discussion, end with prayer.

✦ Closing

Before the girls leave, encourage them to complete the Share Your Story challenge (p. 43). Also encourage them to dig into the five days of Going Deeper devotions included in the book (pp. 44-53).

✤ Welcome (5 minutes)

Greet girls as they arrive and ask them to share highlights from their week. Allow them to share any thoughts or questions from this past week's Going Deeper devotions.

✤ Video (10 minutes)

Watch the Session Four video (included in the DVD Kit). Allow for discussion afterward.

✤ Opening Illustration/Activity (10 minutes)

Direct girls' attention to the miniature "connect-the-dots" picture on page 56. Talk about the concept of connect-the-dots activities—in order to complete the picture, you must connect the dots in order by number. Ask if anyone can guess what the picture is just by looking at the random dots on the page. Allow them to trace out the numbers and see who can finish the picture first. The final image will be the sunshine icon we designated as our symbol for hope.

Transitional statement: As we dig into chapter 4, we will discover several topics that Paul addressed with the Thessalonians: sexual purity, relationships, grieving, death, future. When you look at these topics, it appears to be a laundry list of complex issues that need to be dealt with separately. However, Paul connected the dots for them on a spiritual level. As Christ-followers, we don't live segmented lives—everything is woven together by our faith in Christ. The fact is, when the resurrected Christ transforms our hearts, He connects the dots in such a way that every aspect of our lives is impacted by Him.

✤ Between the Lines (20 minutes)

Read through the historical context and word studies used throughout the session (pp. 57-59). Highlight the information you want to cover with the girls as you study and prepare. Use the questions in this section to spark discussion. Encourage girls to use the Scripture page (p. 55) to underline, circle, and draw in the margin as you go through the passage.

✤ Reflect and Respond (10 minutes)

Consider splitting girls into smaller groups or pairs to discuss the application questions and challenges in this section (p. 59). After a few minutes of discussion, end with prayer.

✤ Closing

Before the girls leave, encourage them to complete the Share Your Story challenge (p. 59). Also encourage them to dig into the five days of Going Deeper devotions included in the book (pp. 60-69).

❖ Welcome (5 minutes)

Greet girls as they arrive and ask them to share highlights from their week. Allow them to share any thoughts or questions from this past week's Going Deeper devotions.

❖ Video (10 minutes)

Watch the Session Five video (included in the DVD Kit). Allow for discussion afterward.

❖ Opening Illustration/Activity (10 minutes)

There are a lot of great illustrations to set the stage for a lesson on light versus darkness. Below are a few ideas.

- ✦ Use a computer to look up images of stars against the night sky (or you could physically go outside and view the night sky if possible).
- ✦ Give the girls flashlights to use as the only source of light in the room for the duration of the lesson.
- ✦ Display a Lite-Brite® set in the corner with the Scripture 1 Thessalonians 5:4-5 written in Lite-Brite pegs.

Whatever visual you choose to use to reinforce the imagery of light versus darkness, allow the girls to discuss the spiritual implications of the illustration.

Transitional statement: Even in darkness, we can see glimpses of light piercing through the black backdrop. Today we are going to look at the picture of night and day that Paul gave the Thessalonians. He used familiar imagery as an analogy for the two ways of living in reality of the Day of the Lord.

❖ Between the Lines (20 minutes)

Read through the historical context and word studies used throughout the session (pp. 72-74). Highlight the information you want to cover with the girls as you study and prepare. Use the questions in this section to spark discussion. Encourage girls to use the Scripture page (p. 71) to underline, circle, and draw in the margin as you go through the passage.

❖ Reflect and Respond (10 minutes)

Consider splitting girls into smaller groups or pairs to discuss the application questions and challenges in this section (p. 75). After a few minutes of discussion, end with prayer.

❖ Closing

Before the girls leave, encourage them to complete the Share Your Story challenge (p. 75). Also encourage them to dig into the five days of Going Deeper devotions included in the book (pp. 76-85).

❖ Welcome (5 minutes)

Greet girls as they arrive and ask them to share highlights from their week. Allow them to share any thoughts or questions from this past week's Going Deeper devotions.

❖ Video (10 minutes)

Watch the Session Six video (included in the DVD Kit). Allow for discussion afterward.

❖ Opening Illustration/Activity (10 minutes)

As you prepare for this session, think agriculture and plant growth. This is a great picture for girls to have in mind as they think about what it means to have a faith that flourishes. For an illustration, you could bring a houseplant or you could get really crazy and have this session meet in a garden. If you can't physically change locations, you could print off pictures of plants and have those as decorations around the room when girls arrive.

Once you get started, instruct girls to read about the fake "Plantstagram" app on page 88. Allow them to have some fun imagining what this app would be like. The more you can get girls to connect with the imagery of a plant, the easier it will be for them to visualize their faith with the characteristics of a plant. Encourage them to use the blank Instagram-like box on the page to sketch a plant, flower, or vegetation of some sort that they have personally planted, picked, or taken care of. Guide them to use the "status box" to describe the outcome of that particular plant/flower/tree/vegetation story.

Transitional statement: As we "dig" in to this second letter from Paul, think about the Thessalonians' growth like a horticulturist might approach a plant. We will look at what it takes to foster spiritual growth and what could potentially threaten that growth.

❖ Between the Lines (20 minutes)

Read through the historical context and word studies used throughout the session (pp. 89-90). Highlight the information you want to cover with the girls as you study and prepare. Use the questions in this section to spark discussion. Encourage girls to use the Scripture page (p. 87) to underline, circle, and draw in the margin as you go through the passage.

❖ Reflect and Respond (10 minutes)

Consider splitting girls into smaller groups or pairs to discuss the application questions and challenges in this section (p. 91). After a few minutes of discussion, end with prayer.

❖ Closing

Before the girls leave, encourage them to complete the Share Your Story challenge (p. 91). Also encourage them to dig into the five days of Going Deeper devotions included in the book (pp. 92-101).

✦ Welcome (5 minutes)

Greet girls as they arrive and ask them to share highlights from their week. Allow them to share any thoughts or questions from this past week's Going Deeper devotions.

✦ Video (10 minutes)

Watch the Session Seven video (included in the DVD Kit). Allow for discussion afterward.

✦ Opening Illustration/Activity (10 minutes)

In the center of the room, place a large manila folder with a fake operation name written in red and the word CONFIDENTIAL stamped on the front. Consider wearing sunglasses and a Bluetooth® ear piece to help create the illusion of a CIA agent meeting. As girls enter the room, allow them to create their own secret agent name. When you are ready to begin, instruct the group to turn to page 104 and answer the questions in the Intro section.

Transitional statement: The image of a highly trained agent will be helpful as we prepare to study 2 Thessalonians chapter two. In this passage, Paul called attention to the false teachers and faulty information being used to deceive them. The church of Thessalonica was under attack and Paul wanted these young believers to recognize the battle they were in.

✦ Between the Lines (20 minutes)

Read through the historical context and word studies used throughout the session (pp. 104-106). Highlight the information you want to cover with the girls as you study and prepare. Use the questions in this section to spark discussion. Encourage girls to use the Scripture page (p. 103) to underline, circle, and draw in the margin as you go through the passage.

✦ Reflect and Respond (10 minutes)

Consider splitting girls into smaller groups or pairs to discuss the application questions and challenges in this section (p. 107). After a few minutes of discussion, end with prayer.

✦ Closing

Before the girls leave, encourage them to complete the Share Your Story challenge (p. 107). Also encourage them to dig into the five days of Going Deeper devotions included in the book (pp. 108-117).

✤ Welcome (5 minutes)

Greet girls as they arrive and ask them to share highlights from their week. Allow them to share any thoughts or questions from this past week's Going Deeper devotions.

✤ Video (10 minutes)

Watch the Session Eight video (included in the DVD Kit). Allow for discussion afterward.

✤ Opening Illustration/Activity (10 minutes)

As an illustration, consider placing a piggy bank in the center of the room surrounded by various coins. Ask them to identify what message is imprinted on every U.S. coin. The answer is, *In God We Trust.* Lead girls to open their books to page 120 and participate in an old fashioned art activity—a coin rub. Instruct them to place a coin under that page and rub across the indention of the coin with a pencil until the image appears. The image may be blurry, but it will serve as a reminder of what it means to live by that statement, *In God We Trust.*

Transitional statement: Think about how many people carry the phrase *In God We Trust* around in purses, pockets, backpacks, even the crevices of couches and car seats, without even considering the implications of that statement. For weeks now we've been looking at a particular group of believers who put their faith in God and trusted Him with their lives. As we wrap up this study, we must consider what it means for us to do the same.

✤ Between the Lines (20 minutes)

Read through the historical context and word studies used throughout the session (pp. 121-122). Highlight the information you want to cover with the girls as you study and prepare. Use the questions in this section to spark discussion. Encourage girls to use the Scripture page (p. 119) to underline, circle, and draw in the margin as you go through the passage.

✤ Reflect and Respond (10 minutes)

Consider splitting girls into smaller groups or pairs to discuss the application questions and challenges in this section (p. 123). After a few minutes of discussion, end with prayer.

✤ Closing

Before the girls leave, encourage them to complete the Share Your Story challenge (p. 123). Also encourage them to dig into the five days of Going Deeper devotions included in the book (pp. 124-133).

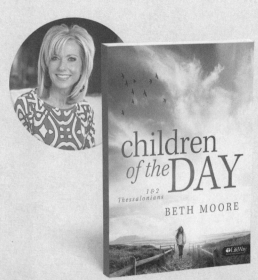